D0336592

WHAT PLANET AM I ON?

Also by Shaun Ryder

Twisting My Melon

WHAT PLANET AM I ON?

Shaun Ryder

Constable • London

Constable & Robinson Ltd
55–56 Russell Square
London WC1B 4HP
www.constablerobinson.com

First published in the UK by Constable,
an imprint of Constable & Robinson Ltd, 2013

A copy of the British Library Cataloguing in Publication
Data is available from the British Library

ISBN 978-1-78033-949-8 (hardback)
ISBN 978-1-78033-957-3 (ebook)

Printed and bound by CPI Group (UK) Ltd, Croydon, CR0 4YY

1 3 5 7 9 10 8 6 4 2

To my wife and children

Acknowledgements

My thanks go to my wife, Joanne Ryder, and my children, for being there and being my backbone. I will always love you all; big thanks to my manager, Warren Askew, for making this happen, and special thanks to his wife Hayley and the kids for looking after me when I'm down south; to my mum and dad and family; my mother-in-law, Grannybag Joan; Amelia Ryder, the first doctor in the Ryder family; Peter Diver; my personal trainer, Gavin Kelly; Matt, Pat, Karen and Sam; Maria Carroll; Uncle Tom and Aunty Mary, RIP; Nikki Stevens; a big thank you to my fans for their support over the years; Andreas Campomar, Jo Stansall and Charlotte Macdonald at Constable & Robinson, for publishing the book and all their hard work on it. Sorry if the changes came in late; Matthew Hamilton, my literary agent at Aitken Alexander Associates; thanks to Wayne Derrick, the director of my TV series, Emma Pound, the AP, and everyone else who worked on the series; Pancho and Jorge, our drivers and fixers in Chile . . . and everyone I met along the way; and a massive thanks to Luke Bainbridge, who accompanied me on the UFO trip and helped me put pen to paper to record.

Contents

INTRODUCTION

My Lifelong Fascination with UFOs

I'VE NEVER QUITE understood why some people think it's weird to be interested in UFOs.

The question for me is not why would you be interested in UFOs, but why *wouldn't* you be interested in UFOs?

It's something that's fascinated me all my life, particularly since I first saw one as a teenager. Believe me, if you see a UFO it sticks with you. I've never forgotten that day. I've forgotten big chunks of my life, especially some of the heady years, well decades really, when I was on the road with Happy Mondays and Black Grape. But I've never forgotten what happened that morning (which we'll get to later). It's been with me ever since.

I know some people assume that UFOs are something that I got into in my wild, partying days with the Mondays, but that's not the case. My fascination with UFOs started well before then, when I was a kid, and as I've got older, and my partying days are pretty much over, if anything my fascination with UFOs has just got stronger. I believed there was life out there way before I ever took drugs, and I had my first two encounters when I was young. I never actually had an encounter or saw anything extraterrestrial in the years I was partying.

I can see why people might make that assumption because it's a classic late-night conversation you might have. Those long nights when one of the things you start thinking about is what does it all mean? Is this all there is? Is there more to life than this? Are we alone in this universe or are there other things out there?

I've never really talked about it in public before. Well, certainly not in any depth. I think a lot of people know that I saw a UFO when I was younger, particularly as it was featured in the film *24 Hour Party People* – although it was portrayed very differently in the film to how it happened in real life. Not that anyone should believe what happens in that film. I liked *24 Hour Party People*, I thought it was a good film, but it's a film; that's not *me*. That's not a documentary about my life. The Shaun Ryder in the film is a caricature. It amazes me how people just swallow everything whole.

So there was a little scene in the film, which a lot of people will have seen, and it's been mentioned in interviews over the years but only ever in passing. I might have done an interview with *NME* or someone, but it usually goes something like:

'So, I believe you've seen a UFO, Shaun?'

'Yeah.'

'Was you on drugs at the time?'

'No.'

'Was you drunk at the time?'

'No.'

. . . and that's about it. Seriously. That's about as investigative as most of these journalists get. They've got a student mentality, most of them. That's what I have to put up with. They probably want a rock 'n' roll story that they can tell their mates down the pub involving Shaun Ryder. Get a life, mate. Maybe if I had told them, 'Yes, I was off my head when I saw it', then they would have wanted to know more. But I've honestly never really been asked much more than that about it.

After I came runner-up on *I'm a Celebrity . . . Get Me Out of Here!* and then my autobiography *Twisting My Melon* did well, I got loads of offers to do TV shows, and my manager Warren had untold meetings with various production companies and TV channels about different shows. I got asked to do *Strictly* but that clashed with *I'm a Celebrity . . .* so I didn't do it. I did do *All Star Mr & Mrs* with my wife Joanne, which was great, and we won £8,000 for our local school charity. But a lot of the other proposals we got were more Shaun Ryder rock'n'roll clichés, which to me were just boring. It makes me laugh how these people sit in brain-storming meetings in production companies and that's the best they can come up with.

But then, along the way, my manager Warren said, 'What would *you* like to do, Shaun?' I've spent most of the last thirty years with people asking me to do things – Will you do this gig? Will you do this interview? Will you go on this chat show? So it was refreshing to be asked for my ideas.

I told them I'd like to make a TV series and a book investigating UFOs and everyone thought it was a great idea. So all of a sudden we're on. Bingo! Next thing I know I'm asked to draw up a list of people I want to meet and places I want to go, and a year later here we are. It was a pretty wild road trip, and I learnt a lot. I met some fascinating people on the road and a few nutters, it has to be said, but I also got a bit more than I bargained for.

CHAPTER 1

Close Encounters of the
Ryder Kind

AS A LITTLE kid I wouldn't say I was obsessed, but I was definitely fascinated by the sky at night and space. When we lived in our house on Cemetery Road in Salford and I was about six years old, me and Our Paul shared a room and bunk beds. I was always on the top bunk and Our Paul was on the bottom bunk. I would spend all night looking out at the night sky, just staring up at the stars and into space.

I kind of knew from that age that we definitely weren't alone in the universe. I didn't talk about it to everyone, but like most kids that age I had a very open, fertile mind, and it was something I thought about quite a lot when I was lying on that top bunk looking up at the stars – the fact that there was definitely more stuff going on out there. It wasn't something that someone put in my head or anything. I wasn't a nut, do you know what I mean? I'm not sure there were such things as space geeks back then, but I was fascinated by it.

No one in my family was massively into it, although I know my dad did believe that we weren't alone in the universe. We just had a couple of those little conversations about it that you have between father and son. My dad certainly wasn't a sci-fi nut either, but his philosophy was simply that there was other life out there somewhere, and those people who thought there wasn't and just dismissed the idea would one day end up looking as stupid as those people in olden days who thought that if you rowed your boat out far enough you would fall off the end of the world because it was flat. My dad was pretty philosophical about it, but that was just his personal opinion – he wasn't obsessed and he didn't read books on it or anything. It was just one of the things that me and him used to talk about when I was a little kid. Not around the table when we were having our tea, but just me and him having a little chat.

I was always bang into all sorts of space gear as a kid – I loved *Star Trek*. I was quite young when it started in the sixties and when I first got into it as a kid I used to call it 'Spock'. He was just the most identifiable thing in it to a young kid, wasn't he? With his ears and a name like that? He was super intelligent as well. So I'd always be asking my mam and dad, 'When's Spock on?' or 'Can we watch Spock?'

But the biggest thing that really got everyone thinking

about space travel when I was a kid was man landing on the moon. That happened in 1969, when I was seven years old, and I remember it quite clearly. It was a huge deal at the time, and I remember my dad went out and got us our first colour telly for it. It was a big old thing, a rented television with a meter on the back where you had to put 10p in. Then the rental guy would come round and empty the meter every now and then. Imagine that now? Having to stick 10p in the back of your telly if you want to watch *Coronation Street*.

The moon landings were obviously a huge deal at the time – it was as big as the World Cup or something. It was televised and they disrupted all the normal scheduling to show it. When I went to school that was all anyone was talking about.

There were also a few huge sci-fi movies that came out in the late seventies when I was a teenager, especially *Close Encounters of the Third Kind* and *Star Wars*. At the time I thought *Close Encounters* was a great movie, but I thought *Star Wars* was just fantasy nonsense; it's like a comedy Wild West movie set in space. Ridiculous. I was fifteen when it came out in 1977 and I just didn't enjoy all that saving-the-Princess routine and battling-for-the-Federation bollocks. It was just not for me. Garbage. I thought *Close Encounters* was a much better movie at the time, and I still do. To me it was more real than *Star Wars*. So I'm not one of those nerds on space, those sci-fi nuts who just love everything. When the *Star Wars* prequels came out in the noughties, with Ewan McGregor and

Samuel L Jackson in them, I tried watching them, but I still wasn't having it. Ollie, one of our kids, was a teenager then, and he had all the *Star Wars* figures and was bang into it, so I thought I would give it another go, but nah. It's just not my scene. *Star Wars* is a world that you either buy into as a kid or you don't, you know what I mean? It's like my little girls, Pearl and Lulu, are not into *The Hobbit* or *Lord of the Rings*, and they're not interested in *Harry Potter* either. Most kids love *Harry Potter*, but they're not having it. I was the same with *Star Wars*.

So like I say, as a kid I loved gazing at the stars at night and the moon landings, but I wasn't a total nut or anything. Having said that, back in the late sixties there wasn't much around to go overboard on anyway. *Doctor Who* was OK, I'd usually watch it if it was on, but I wasn't mad for it. I liked *Thunderbirds*, thought that was OK, but *Captain Scarlet* was better.

Star Trek, or 'Spock', was the main one for me when I was growing up. I've stuck with *Star Trek* over the years as well – we've had a long relationship. Years later, after I started Black Grape with Kermit, who was a big *Star Trek* nut as well (he just happened to be, that's not why we started the band together), we were asked to go on a *Star Trek* night on BBC2. We had to talk about how we first got into it and what we thought about different characters, and our opinion on *Star Trek: The Next Generation* and all that. I remember when *The Next Generation* started in the mid-eighties. When I first heard they were going to do it, I thought, 'Awww, bollocks!' I just thought it was a really bad idea, and it was going to be terrible and ruin *Star Trek* for everyone. But after watching the first few episodes I admit I was totally wrong. *The Next Generation* just blew me away.

A lot of the stuff that happens in *Star Trek* is very believable to me. I have this theory that if we as humans can imagine something, then it's achievable, you know what I mean? Kermit was with me on that as well, all the way. My favourite episode of *The Next Generation* is called 'Elementary, Dear Data', when Professor Moriarty, who was Sherlock Holmes's enemy or nemesis, tries to take over the ship, or at least a hologram of him does. What happens is that Commander Data generally has a pretty stressful time on the Starship *Enterprise*, dealing with all these extremely futuristic life forms and people from other planets, and making sure that Warp Factor Three is safe for the ozone and all sorts of stuff. So when he needs to just kick back, he goes up to the Holodeck, and in this episode he gets involved in the re-enactment of a Sherlock Holmes mystery. It's called the Holodeck because that's where the holograms are, but to Data it's more of a holiday deck, a Holideck, as that's where he goes for a bit of time out. I tell you what, if we had something like that in real life, drug use would go down by about 99 per cent – if we had a hologram world we could escape into and take a break from real life. Basically Moriarty just takes the piss all the way through the episode and it's great. Check it out if you haven't seen it, it's a great episode.

★

So I was always interested in space and the possibility of life on other planets, but then in the late seventies I had two personal encounters with UFOs that changed my life and changed my thinking on it.

The first one happened at th' Height – Irlams o' th' Height – which is a place near us when we were growing up. I was stood at a bus stop at th' Height at about 9 p.m. at night. It was late summer so it was just going dark. I'd been out with a couple of pals of mine from school who lived at th' Height and I was waiting to get a bus back up to Little Hulton, where I lived.

I looked up and just saw hundreds of lights across the sky, hundreds of them. My first thought was, 'Fuck me, are we being invaded?!' It was amazing. I'd never seen anything like it in my life. There were hundreds of these lights moving across the sky and they looked like craft. It scared me a little bit at first, but then I actually found it quite calming. I think if an adult saw something like that for the first time, they might be quite scared, but because I was a kid I wasn't as frightened. As a kid you're more innocent and naive, aren't you? But as an adult you might sense the danger a bit more.

Quite a few other people saw it and it was reported in the *Salford Journal* or *Reporter*. Some spokesperson for the authorities, the head of police or Salford Council or something, blamed it on the floodlights of Salford Rugby Club going haywire, going bonkers, which was absolute bullshit. I remember reading the paper at the time, thinking, '*You what?* Bullshit! Who you trying to kid?' I knew what the lights at Salford rugby ground looked like, because I'd grown up there and I used to go and watch the rugby sometimes with my granddad and Our Paul. What I saw that night looked fuck-all like Salford's floodlights. The lights I saw were different colours for a start and were slow-moving objects, and there were what looked like hundreds of them moving slowly across the sky.

Over the past decade or so, as I've got into watching documentaries on the History and Discovery channels and checking stuff out on YouTube, I've seen clips of similar things and I've been like, 'Wow! That's what I saw that night!' I'm now pretty sure it was hundreds of craft moving slowly across the sky.

A few months later, probably late September or early October 1978, I had my second incident or encounter. I'd just left school by that time and started work as a post boy. I was on the 8 to 3.30 shift at the post office, so I was walking to the bus stop on Hilton Lane about 6.40 a.m. to get on the bus to work and it was still dark – that time of the morning when the dawn is just creeping in. There was a little lad who must have been about eleven or twelve in front of me, also walking to the bus stop. He must have been at one of the grammar schools in town, De La Salle or Manchester Grammar. As I'm walking to the bus stop I looked up and saw this object just flash across the sky in front of me at about 10,000 miles an hour. I watched it zip across and then I looked at the little lad, and he was watching it as well.

As we reached the bus stop, we both just stood there watching this object, this thing. And it was fucking spellbinding. I'd never seen anything like it. This object was shooting across the sky . . . sssssccchhhhhOOOOm-mmmMMMMMM . . . zzzzzoZZZZOOOOOOOOOM-MMMMM . . . in this mad zigzag pattern from one side to the other, at what seemed about 10,000 miles an hour. Then it would stop and then kind of hang about in one spot for a little bit, and then it was off again . . . ssssssssshhhhhhh . . . zigzagging back across the sky again. Then it might hover about for a little bit, and then again …sssssccchhhhhhOOOOmmmmMMMM MM . . . zzzzzoZZZZOOOOOOOOOMMMMMM . . . zigzagging back across the sky again.

And then all of a sudden it just did one.

Got off at about 10,000 miles an hour.

Disappeared.

Gone.

It's hard to describe it, or even say how big it was, because it was pretty far away. We were in Salford, but I reckon this craft could have even been above the moors between Bolton and Rochdale. To me, it looked like a star moving about, but just lower down. It's hard to get perspective on something when it's in the sky and moving that fast.

Again, like my first incident, other people had seen it as well because there were some reports in the press about people seeing similar things as far away as Bolton and even Todmorden in Yorkshire. But that makes sense, doesn't it? If this craft was flitting about at 10,000 miles an hour, then when I was watching it zigzag across the sky it could well have been flitting between the Pennines and Liverpool.

Aside from my two incidents, there were also quite a few other reports of similar types of activity in the skies near me around the same time. The north-west seemed to be a bit of a hotbed at the time. Farmers saw things. Even police officers have gone on record saying that they saw similar things. It wasn't just me, little Shaun Ryder in Salford, who was seeing things. Loads of people from all walks of life, from bus drivers to lawyers, reported seeing similar things.

Now, the first time I saw something – all those different lights in the sky I mentioned earlier – I definitely knew it wasn't the rugby lights that the local paper used as an explanation. But you do think to yourself, 'You know what? I know it wasn't fucking rugby lights, I know there was something weird going on there, and I clocked it, but maybe there *is* some weird, non-UFO, explanation for it. Maybe it was some freakish optical illusion, or some sort of mini Northern Lights show over Salford.'

But the second time? Nah. I definitely saw something flying around at 10,000 miles an hour, zigzagging around the sky, completely defying physics or what any manmade craft could do. It was definitely a craft of some kind and it certainly wasn't a manmade craft.

Close Encounters of the Third Kind or *Star Wars* hadn't come out at the time – they came out just after my encounter. So it's not as if I'd been to the pictures and floated back home with these visions in my head and conjured it up. I was just on my way to work, freezing my balls off at six a.m. in the morning, and I saw this craft. Not just me, but the little kid that was in front of me as well.

After the craft had disappeared that morning, I got on the bus and went into work and I told everyone about it. No one said, 'Were you tripping?' or 'Are you sure you weren't just stoned?' or anything like that. I hadn't taken acid or anything at that age, and that drug culture wasn't around then either, back in the late seventies, or at least it wasn't widespread. Acid wouldn't have been in the vocabulary of your average postman back then. There was a bit of weed flying around the post office, but that was about it.

I've never forgotten that day. As I've said, I've forgotten days, weeks, months, years and, let's face it, decades of my life, but I've never forgotten that morning. Something like that sticks in your head, believe me.

★

When you have seen something like I did, a craft flying about defying physics, it makes you think about things differently. Later, when I saw films like *Close Encounters of the Third Kind* or *Star Wars*, I did think to myself, 'Well, where do they get their ideas from for these films?' It's not all straight from the imagination of whoever wrote the film, is it? Not all from the mind of a geezer sat in a room at his desk, staring at the wall, chewing his pencil waiting for inspiration. I'm a big one for believing that information is leaked to us through TV programmes and films – through the news, through all sorts.

Steven Spielberg apparently has friends in the military who have told him classified stuff which he then uses as inspiration in his movies. I read an interview once where someone asked him about it, saying, 'You know some people believe you're actually a government agent for aliens because of *Close Encounters of the Third Kind* and *ET*?' And Spielberg replied, 'I'm part of a government conspiracy to make America and the world conducive to accepting an alien neighbour? Great!'

The producer Jamie Shandera made a documentary about Spielberg just as *ET* came out, and said Spielberg told him there was a private screening of *ET* at the White House for Ronald and Nancy Reagan. At the end of the film, the President leant over, tapped Spielberg on the shoulder and quietly said to him, 'You know, there aren't six people in this room who know how true this really is.'

After my first two incidents, I didn't have any similar experiences for years. Decades. There was one incident in Germany with the re-formed Happy Mondays in about 2006, when we thought we might have seen a UFO, but that was slightly different. This wasn't the original line-up of the Mondays, but one I had for a few years in the noughties. We had a very weird experience one night on tour, but I'm pretty sure I can discount that as being more of less just down to the substances that were being consumed. There were a lot of weird people around us at a weird festival, smoking a weird substance, which triggered off a very weird experience.

There were some German dudes there who were real mushroom and dope aficionados and collectors, and they had just been to the Amazon rainforest and brought some stuff back with them. I realized afterwards it was a drug called DMT, which I'd heard about before. I think Bez and his ex-missus were the first people I knew to take it. Its proper name is Dimethyltryptamine (I had to Google that) and it's a natural psychedelic drug. It occurs in plants and there are also traces of it in our bodies. Depending on how much you take, it can give you a proper, full-on immersive psychedelic trip. Loads of South American, Amazonian and American Indian tribes have been taking it for centuries, it's part of their culture. Shamans use it in ceremonies. In the late nineties, dear old Tony Wilson was asked to make a TV show where he went to South America and took this drug to see what happened. I didn't know about it until he came back, quite pleased with himself, and said, 'I've been to the Amazon rainforest and taken a drug even you lot haven't tried.' And I was like, 'Nah, Bez has had it, Tony. Our mate brought some back off his holidays.' Poor Tony was a bit gutted.

There was a good documentary made about it a couple

of years ago called *DMT: The Spirit Molecule*, which is on Netflix and well worth watching. In the documentary, they have scientists who talk about taking DMT and going on trips out to the universe. They're also talking about how they might use it in medical science as well. They all agree it's much more than a drug experience. It opens your mind and helps you understand life and death and all sorts. Lots of people who've taken it say you can see the life around plants, almost like the aura of plants.

DMT seems like a really positive thing to me, but the thing is when you're prepared for that sort of trip then you're ready for it, aren't you? You get yourself in the right mindset. But when you're just at a festival and someone passes you something and you don't know what it is, you just think it's something relatively harmless, so you crack on and then you don't know what's fucking hit you. BOOOOOM! All of a sudden we were in this really, really intense psychotropic mind-bending trip, which was much deeper and more intense than any acid I've ever taken. We were certain we could read each other's minds. We were sat there in this room, absolutely out of it, convinced we were mind-reading, like a scene straight out of a sci-fi film.

I was sat there looking at Johnny, and in my head I'm thinking, 'Right, I'm not talking now, Johnny, OK? And you're not talking either, but nod if you can understand me . . .'

And Johnny nodded, which was just fucking mind-blowing.

Thing is, in reality I was saying all this out loud. We only *thought* we weren't talking.

Then Johnny would do the same to me. He was thinking, 'Right, now let's see if you can read my mind. Nod if you can understand me, Shaun.' And I thought I could hear what he was thinking, so I nodded, and it just blew our minds. The DMT had fucked us up so much we thought we had super powers.

I have a really, really strong mind when it comes to hallucinogenics and things. When me and Bez first met we spent a year doing acid together every day, and I always had a strong enough mind to separate what was tripping and what was real life. Even when me and Bez would be tripping in the fields, and we were looking up at the clouds which were turning into Greek gods and climbing down out of the sky and talking to us – even then I had a strong enough mind to say, 'No, this is a trip, this is not really happening.' And even then we never saw a UFO.

But that incident with the DMT in Germany even threw me for a bit. That DMT stuff was something else. But as I say, that night was just a weird drug experience more than anything. So even though we thought we might have experienced some kind of alien mind-fuck that night, I'd definitely put anything out of the ordinary that happened down to the chemicals.

The reason I'm telling you all this is that I want to make it absolutely clear that despite what people might think, my interest in UFOs is nothing to do with drug experiences. It predates that, it goes back to when I was a kid, and it's still with me now, long after I've stopped partying like I used to.

CHAPTER 2

The Truth is Out There

I'VE GOT A pretty inquisitive mind. I wouldn't say I'm a conspiracy theorist, but I definitely don't believe everything that the government or the media tell us either. I don't believe what politicians or the authorities are telling us half the time. And I don't believe half the stories you read about so-called celebrities, so I definitely don't believe everything that's said, or not said, about UFOs or the existence of life out there.

I find it funny when individuals get into power and they're really interested to find out more about UFOs. I tend to find whoever it is, be it the President of America or the British Prime Minister, gets into office and says, 'Right, show me the UFO file.' Then it generally goes quiet – you never hear anything after that. One of two things happens: either they keep knocking on doors and getting no answer, because even if you're the President or the Prime Minister there's some top secret department who won't give up all their secrets to you. Or perhaps sometimes they do go, 'Here y'are then, here's the UFO file', and Obama or Tony Blair or whoever it is goes, 'Bloody hell, right-o, maybe we better keep schtum about this.'

Either way, once they get in power, they seem to keep quiet about it.

Most people know about the most famous UFO occurrences like the Roswell incident. That was what kicked off popular UFO culture, if you like. Roswell is to ufology what Elvis at Sun Studios is to rock'n'roll, you know what I mean? Ever since then, the public has been fascinated by UFOs. Since I first heard about the Roswell case, I've been gripped by it.

My opinion on Roswell has changed over time. I've always been open to suggestions and up for learning more about possible theories on UFOs, which is one of the reasons I wanted to make the TV series and write this book. I watched one programme about Roswell that made a good case for suggesting it was all tied up with the beginnings of the cold war and nuclear power, and the Americans were trying to explain away new technology they were developing. There's also the other explanation they came up with that it was some new-fangled weather balloon that confused the fuck out of the people who found it because they had never seen such an advanced material, so they thought it was something from another planet. It seemed a pretty convincing argument, and I was having it. But then I did also like the argument that it was a bit of a blag by the Americans to cover up some nuclear experiment – that they would rather have the general public half believing there was a UFO cover-up than the Russians finding out what was really going on, which was that they were developing some new spy plane technology or something. So for a while I was more inclined to believe that perhaps it was a US military cover-up of some kind and the whole alien thing was just a smokescreen.

Then I saw another documentary which showed some other evidence and a new way of looking at it, which made me think again and come back round to thinking, 'Nah, something definitely happened at Roswell. There was definitely some contact with an alien race that those fuckers in charge don't want us knowing about.' Nurses who worked there later came out and swore blind that they were there when autopsies were done on little bodies. So that's where I'm at now with Roswell. I'm back to thinking that something *definitely* went down there.

When the US started their 'Star Wars' programme under Ronald Reagan, obviously your average man on the street got even more interested in what was happening out there in space. Now they've abandoned it, but I don't think that's stopped the general public's interest.

I think young kids are particularly fascinated by UFOs. Especially now they're not being told, like I was, that there is *no* life out there; they're being taught that water has been found on Mars, and that there *may* be life out there somewhere and that there are planets similar to Earth, that could sustain life, being discovered all the time.

I talk to my kids about UFOs and whether there is other life out there, just as my dad used to talk to me when I was a kid. I've talked to them about what I've seen. Their response was, 'Why were they here, Dad?' I said, 'They're probably coming to check up on us, to see how we're doing, to make sure we're all right.' And they were happy with that. I also talk to my wife Joanne about it, and she's very much of the same opinion as me that there is definitely life out there.

If you look back at history, most things that humans have thought about have gone on to be invented. Most things that you think about become reality. Someone thought about photography one day and then it became real. Someone thought about moving pictures one day and it became real. Someone thought about landing on the moon, it became real.

That sort of stuff fascinates me – how the mind works and changes reality. Like the cat-in-the-box theory. It's called the Schrödinger's cat theory. It's a bit too complex for me to explain, but look it up – it's to do with our influence on everything around us and how we affect reality.

★

I think we're all aerials or antennae in a way, and we all tune into and pick up signals from people who are similar to us, and we attract people who think in the same way and believe the same sort of things. That's how we end up getting drawn to certain people. With Happy Mondays, our drummer Gaz Whelan was always bang into UFO sort of stuff, and we would chat about it for hours when we were on tour. Bez also has a really inquisitive mind. I'm sure you all know the boggle-eyed caricature of Bez, which everyone loves, but anyone who's ever sat down and had a chat with Bez, when he's not off his head, will tell you that he's a really intelligent and inquisitive guy. He contradicts himself all the time, on everything and anything, often in the same sentence. But he's an interested, and interesting, dude.

Like I said earlier, Kermit from Black Grape is also fascinated by things like this, which is one of the things we bonded over. Well, along with the fact that we both had quite healthy drug habits at the time. Too Nice Tom, a good friend of mine who is a boxing trainer and directed *The Grape Tapes*, a film about Black Grape, is the same. Too Nice Tom is another geezer who has a very inquisitive mind, and me and him could sit there all day talking and debating about all kinds of things.

I began to investigate more for myself when I started using the internet and sites like YouTube over the last few years. I only became internet friendly, or computer-literate I suppose would be the proper term for it, about four years ago. I never had a bloody computer until I was forty-five. They didn't exist when we were kids, obviously. The first arcades had started coming out that had *Space Invaders* and *Pac Man* and that, but not home computers. Then when I was in a band for twenty years, touring the world, I never really needed a computer. When you're in a band you have a tour manager who organizes everything for you and basically runs your life. You don't need to be going on the internet and checking your flight times or anything. All we needed to do was try to be in hotel reception for whatever time and a car would be there to pick us up.

I remember way back in 1995, when the first Black Grape album came out, me and Kermit had to go down to London and do a load of press interviews and stuff. That was the first time we had to do any press involving the internet. One of the things that we had to do was record one of the first podcasts. I don't think the word podcast had even been invented then, but that's basically what it was, an interview with some geezer that was only put out online, so I suppose it was one of the first podcasts, even if some trendy marketing genius hadn't come up with the actual term yet. The other thing we had to do was a question-and-answer session online with some fans. Some techie guy set us up online and the first thing me and Kermit thought was, 'Bingo, let's talk to girls. Where are the girls?'

I first started to use the internet by myself when I got a phone that had access to the internet on it. This was probably about 2004. At first I just used it for texting.

It took me a little while to get up to speed with that. I remember being on tour with the Mondays in 2006 in the States and we got stopped by the cops, just a routine check, and this cop smacked me on the hand with his truncheon because I was stood there in front of him with my phone in my hand, texting. I couldn't believe it, the cheeky bastard. For once I knew I hadn't even done anything wrong. But the Americans were slower than us to get on to the texting lark, so this cop didn't even know what texting was. I said, 'Ow, what the *fuck* are you doing you *dick*? I'm just texting!' He just saw me with my hand in front of my pants, fiddling around with something, and he made some ridiculous remark about my 'lewd behaviour'. Fuck knows what he thought I was up to but I got a fucking smack on the hand with a truncheon. Nice one. But I've learnt over the years with American cops that their interpretation of what's going on is more important than what is actually happening. It might look to everyone else like you're not doing anything wrong, but if the cop that's in your face interprets it a different way, then you'd better watch out.

After I got the hang of texting, a bit later someone showed me how you could go online, so I started using YouTube and stuff. Then someone showed me how you could use Google to look something up – just type in a name or something and it would show you all the results – and then a bit after that I got a computer at home.

I'm not on Facebook or Twitter or any of that nonsense, though. I can't be doing with all the social media gear. Why would you want to be telling the whole world your personal business like that? You must be crazy to do that. My privacy gets invaded enough, thank you very much. I don't mind doing all the press and TV that comes with the job – in fact, I quite enjoy a lot of it – but the last thing I can imagine doing is sticking a load of personal photos and info up there on the internet for everyone to look at, telling people what you had for tea. You don't know what Facebook or whoever is doing with that information anyway, as all this recent business with the US government shows. We live in enough of a surveillance society as it is; they've got enough info on us all without us giving them a load for free. There are Shaun Ryder pages that are looked after by my management, letting people know about forthcoming gigs and stuff. But there's no Shaun Ryder personal accounts where I upload pics of my steak pudding that I'm having for my tea, or me on a day out with the kids, and there never will be. It's just not for me.

One of the most interesting things I saw recently was the ex-Minister of Defence in Canada who came out and made a speech about the fact that extraterrestrials have been visiting our planet for years. The geezer is called Paul Hellyer, and he's not shy when it comes to talking about UFOs – he's been giving it out for years.

The speech was at a conference called the 'Citizen Hearing on Disclosure', which was basically calling for the US government to come clean about UFOs. Or, as they put it, campaigning for 'what the US Congress had failed to do for forty-five years, to seek out the facts surrounding the most important issue of this or any other time – evidence pointing toward an extraterrestrial presence engaging the human race'.

According to old Hellyer, 'aliens are living among us and . . . it is likely at least two of them are working with the US government'. More specifically, Hellyer announced that at least four species of extraterrestrials have been visiting Earth for thousands of years.

He has also called for 'a public disclosure of alien technology obtained during alleged UFO crashes – such as the mysterious 1947 incident in Roswell, New Mexico'. He said, 'not only do we have ET here, we have the capability to take him home'.

Now, I don't necessarily just accept everything that he says because there's some pretty wild stuff there – to say that two different species of aliens are working with the US government – but I absolutely believe that we have the technology and I believe him when he says species have been here.

I do believe contact was first made with aliens in the fifties and sixties and it was covered up. I heard one theory which said that aliens only made contact with Earth after we discovered nuclear power because they could see the harm we could do with it. I could buy into that. I'm not saying I thought aliens were flying around with those stickers in the back windows of their spaceships saying 'Nuclear Power? No Thanks', but I could see that if they knew more than us about it, and knew it was really destructive, they might want to warn us off, especially if our messing around could end up affecting them as well.

There's an American dude called Robert Hastings who has been researching UFOs for years. He reckons aliens 'tried to warn the US and Russia that they were playing with fire during the Cold War'. He's gathered witness statements from more than 120 military personnel over the years, claiming to show infiltration of nuclear sites by UFOs. One of those witnesses was Captain Robert Salas, a former US Air Force Ballistic Missile Launch officer, who said he was on duty during a missile disruption incident at Malmstrom Air Force base in Montana in 1967. He said he saw a 'large glowing, pulsating red oval shaped object' hovering over the front gate. He then noticed that the missiles he was overseeing had shut down. 'The indicators for all or nearly all ten missiles showed as red-coloured "fault" lights, which meant that the missiles were disabled and could not be launched.' He was told by his superiors not to discuss the matter.

Does that really seem so bonkers? We know ourselves that we're playing with fire a bit with nuclear power, which is why some people are so against it. So what if there was an alien race out there, who were twice as advanced as us, and they could see what we were messing about with, and they actually knew how dangerous it was? When you put it like that it doesn't seem so crazy, does it? Imagine it. They'd definitely want to take a look at what was going on.

I would love to know the full truth about what governments know, and I set out to find out more while making the TV series and writing this book. But I do believe that if the authorities did turn round and say, 'OK, it's true, we are in contact with aliens', then a lot of people would go bananas. Their heads would explode. Some people would just not be able to get their heads round it at all. It would challenge everything they thought was real.

Look back at when Orson Welles's *The War of the Worlds* was first broadcast back in the thirties. It was a fake live news programme on the radio (this is before TV, remember) about an alien invasion that was supposedly happening. They said at the start that it was fictional, but loads of people switched on later and missed that bit, and totally thought it was for real. People panicked. I think a lot of people still would today.

I do truly believe that there will be an announcement about contact with aliens one day, though. Whether that will be in my lifetime or not, I don't know.

My generation, and the generations before me, were generally brought up being told by the authorities that there is no life on other planets. Now things have changed slightly. We accept that there is water and probably some form of bacterial life on Mars, and most sensible people, including scientists, believe that there is life out there somewhere, if not in this galaxy then in another galaxy. Whether they believe that life has come to visit us on Earth, or will ever come to visit us here, is a different matter, but most of them believe something. I think it's healthier for kids to grow up with that sort of thinking.

Astronomers have found 200 planets in the last six months that are like Earth, apparently – mirror Earths. If there are so many mirror Earths out there, then I think it's pretty obvious that one day we will discover that there is life on one of these planets. Whether we're able to communicate with them, I don't know. On the other hand, there is also the chance that the message will come the other way and they'll get in touch with us.

It's only a matter of time, really.

Mathematically, the universe must be teeming with life.

The truth is out there, as they say. I wouldn't be as daft as to say I'm determined to find it, but I really want to get closer to it.

CHAPTER 3

Ziggy Stardust and Other Spiders from Mars

I'M FAR FROM the first musician to be fascinated by UFOs and life on other planets. From David Bowie to Jimi Hendrix, John Lennon to Robbie Williams, there's a long illustrious history of musicians who have been fascinated by UFOs and space. Maybe it's because we musicians are a bit otherworldly ourselves. Some musicians have even said that they believe they can tap into a cosmic super power that helps them write some of their best songs or produce their best performances on stage. I can see why they might say that, because the inspiration comes from somewhere, and the balls come from somewhere to get up on stage and perform, but I'm not sure I agree that it comes from any cosmic super power. Cynics may say that musicians and rock stars take a lot of drugs, but most of the incidents that I've heard about involving musicians and UFOs or encounters don't involve drugs at all.

When I read John Lennon's account of seeing a UFO above New York City, I totally felt for him when he had to stress that drugs were not involved in the experience at all – just like I've had to.

Over the years, plenty of musicians have also written songs, or even themed whole albums around their obsession with UFOs. I've personally never written a song about UFOs or aliens in all my years with Happy Mondays or Black Grape. But then I very rarely ever write a specific song about anything in particular. Most of my songs I put together like a magpie, dragging together different lines and images that work well together. Probably the closest I came to revealing my extraterrestrial interests was name-checking Neil Armstrong in the Black Grape single 'In the Name of the Father':

> Neil Armstrong, astronaut,
> he had balls bigger than King Kong,
> First big suit on the moon, and he's off to play golf
> hole in one!

But that didn't mean anything really. When we were making the first Black Grape album, me and Kermit would just riff off each other in the studio a lot of the time. We'd both have little snippets and one-liners, and a song would emerge from that.

★

When I was growing up, David Bowie was the main pop star who was writing about space and life on other planets, or certainly the main one who we knew about, the geezer who was speaking to kids like me. But Bowie was far from the first. What did John Lennon say about Elvis? Before anyone did anything, Elvis did everything? Well, that applies to UFOs as well.

There's a well-known story told by Elvis's dad about how there was a big blue light that shone above his house when Elvis was born. Elvis himself came out with some bonkers stuff in his time, but in the last fifteen years of his life he became mates with a woman called Wanda June Hill who recorded some strange interviews with him. There's some debate over these interviews but they've been checked out by a specialist who says it is Elvis.

In one of these interviews he tells old Wanda that he was visited by 'life forms' as a kid. 'I am not of this world,' Elvis told her. 'I am a man, I am a human being now, but what is "me" is not from here. I am from out there . . . you think I am making this up, but it's true – you'll know one day.'

When he was shooting the film *Spinout* in 1966, Elvis started seeing his co-star Deborah Walley at the same time, and told her that he didn't want to spend any time on 'trivialities': 'I got the word. I want to give it to you. I'm not a man. I'm not a woman. I'm a soul, a spirit, a force. I have no interest in anything of this world. I want to live in another dimension entirely.'

Elvis had several UFO encounters including one in the late sixties when he was driving down Route 66 with Larry Geller and Jerry Schilling, two of the 'Memphis Mafia' (which is what they called the hangers-on who were always around Elvis). Elvis saw a 'flying saucer' cross the sky in front of them and get brighter, then do a right-hand turn and just shoot off into the distance. 'That was definitely not a shooting star!' said Elvis. The other two agreed. Jerry pointed out that nothing manmade moved like that and Larry said, 'That thing moved like a flying saucer.' Elvis later told Larry, 'It's ridiculous to think we're the only life with millions of planets in the universe.'

I'm totally with old Elvis on that one. Couldn't agree with you more, mate.

You could spend your life reading about Elvis, and there are quite a few extraterrestrial connections we read about while researching this book and TV series. It didn't stop when he died either – loads of people have claimed to have seen weird lights and phenomena over Graceland since.

I'm not sure where Elton John was coming from when he first saw a picture of Elvis from 'Heartbreak Hotel' and thought he resembled 'a man from Mars'. But I do remember an episode of *The X-Files* where references were made to Elvis's UFO connections. FBI agent Fox Mulder told his partner Dana Scully that he was going on a spiritual journey and then at the end of the show he tips up at Graceland, putting on Elvis shades.

There were lots of incidents with musicians and UFOs in the sixties, which I'm sure your cynics will say was down to the amount of acid that was being taken at the time. I think it was mostly just a case of musicians being fascinated by space and the possibilities of other life out there in the cosmos at the time. In the early sixties there were loads of bands who gave themselves cosmic names like Bill Haley and the Comets, the Telstars, the Zodiacs and others. Everyone knows that the Beatles were first called the Quarrymen, but they also changed their name to Johnny and the Moondogs for a short while. When the Beatles started becoming famous, John Lennon was asked in an interview where the name came from and he said, 'It came in a vision – a man appeared on a flaming pie and said unto us "From this day on you are Beatles with an 'A'."' Most people assumed that 'flaming pie in the sky' referred to a UFO. Paul McCartney also did a solo album in the nineties called *Flaming Pie*.

John Lennon's main UFO incident came much later when he was living in New York. On 23 August 1974, Lennon and May Pang (his assistant who he got together with for a bit when he split from Yoko) saw a UFO from his apartment balcony at the Dakota Building in New York. May later described what happened, saying that John was screaming for her to come out on to the terrace and she saw 'this large, circular object coming towards us. It was shaped like a flattened cone, and on top was a large, brilliant red light, not pulsating as on any of the aircraft we'd see heading for a landing at Newark Airport.' May said they stood there mesmerized, unable to believe what they were seeing.

Lennon and May were naked as apparently it was a hot night.

'Suppose it's looking at us,' May said. 'Maybe they think that everyone who lives on the East Side wanders around naked on their terraces on Friday evening. We look like Adam and Eve.'

The UFO then did one and headed off towards Brooklyn, and Lennon shouted, 'Stop, take me with you!'

May said that all that night, Lennon kept repeating, 'I can't believe it . . . I've seen a flying saucer.'

Lennon had just finished his *Walls and Bridges* album, which came out the next month, and on the liner notes he wrote, 'On the 23rd August 1974 at 9 o'clock I saw a UFO – JL.'

He later referenced the episode in two songs, 'Out of the Blue' from the album *Mind Games* and 'Nobody Told Me' from *Milk and Honey*.

Lennon also had another weird incident that he told Uri Geller about: 'You ain't fuckin' gonna believe this'. Lennon said he was asleep with Yoko at home in the Dakota Building when he woke up because 'there was this blazing light round the door. It was shining through the cracks and the keyhole, like someone was out there with searchlights, or the apartment was on fire.'

Lennon jumped out of bed and opened the door.

'There were these four people out there. They were, like, little. Bug-like. Big bug eyes and little bug mouths and they were scuttling at me like roaches.'

He insisted that he wasn't on drugs when it happened. 'I never saw anything on acid that was as weird as those fuckin' bugs, man.' He said he tried to throw the little people out of his apartment, but they pushed him back just using willpower and telepathy.

Lennon then woke up back in bed and he had a metal, egg-like object in his hand. He gave it to Uri Geller, saying he didn't want to keep it because it was too weird for him: 'If it's my ticket to another planet, I don't want to go there.'

Lennon had an open mind on most things, not just UFOs, which is where I'm coming from too. I remember reading him summing up his attitude: 'I believe in everything until it's disproved. It all exists, even if it's in your mind. Who's to say dreams and nightmares aren't as real as the here and now? Reality leaves quite a lot to the imagination.'

I'm with him on that.

★

The Rolling Stones also have strong UFO connections. Mick Jagger, Marianne Faithfull and a few others were camping at Glastonbury Tor in 1968 when they saw a huge spaceship above them. Marianne Faithfull said at the time that Mick 'wants to know what everyone else is thinking. The New Age grail questers . . . were searching for UFOs, ley lines and other totems of the Age of Aquarius'. Which is all a bit hippy for me. It's pretty well documented that Jagger also thought he saw a UFO during their infamous gig at Altamont, but that's hardly surprising considering all the other shit that was going down that night. Jagger must have been a little spooked at one stage because apparently he even had a UFO detector installed at his mansion!

Keith Richards also said he saw 'several discs' above his house in Sussex in 1968. 'I've seen a few,' Keith said, 'but nothing that any of the ministries would believe. I believe they exist – plenty of people have seen them.'

Jimi Hendrix was also a believer. Hendrix was part American Indian, and so are a lot of people from near me in Salford, believe it or not. Or they could be. At the end of the nineteenth century, a gang of Native Americans came over as part of Buffalo Bill's Wild West Circus and they disappeared when they reached Salford. Turns out they were wanted by the US government on charges of war crimes after they beat General Custer. So when they reached Salford, they just vanished under the arches at Greengate and the locals hid them because they thought they were great warriors, not war criminals. The Native Americans ended up having loads of kids with the locals and a lot of them are buried at Pendleton Church. I'm not making this up. If you look in the graveyard there you'll see gravestones for names like 'Enid', 'Harry' and 'George' and then one for 'Running Water' or something.

I often wonder if that's why people from Salford are a slightly different breed, why we have no fear – because we have a bit of Native American blood in us.

Anyway, old Hendrix reckoned he had been a full-on, full-blooded American Indian in a past life. He also said he experienced astral travel in adulthood. Some of his best-known songs were about space and aliens and their impact on Earth. The oddest incident happened when he was filming his Rainbow Bridge gig in 1970 at the Haleakala Crater on the island of Maui, which even sounds like the right place for a UFO encounter. The crew were trekking through the crater with a load of donkeys carrying all the gear when they suddenly saw a silver disc hovering in the clear sky. Guitarist Merrell Fankhauser said, 'Jimi walked out on the cinder field of an 800 year old lava flow with open arms saying, "Welcome, space brothers!"'

This next bit made me laugh. Fankhauser described how everyone was stunned at seeing the UFO except a film producer who'd been at the whisky and was waddling along on the back of a donkey. He couldn't see a thing and told them all that they were crazy. 'The producer became so upset when people kept pointing to the glowing orb that he fell off the donkey, injured his back, and had to be airlifted by helicopter.'

Another musician, Curtis Knight, said Jimi told him that 'the craft had come down to put its spiritual stamp of approval on the show. He also said that he'd been emotionally and physically recharged by the experience.'

Reg Presley, the lead singer of the Troggs who sang 'Wild Thing', was another one who was bang into UFOs and space. In the mid-1990s, he even had his own TV show called *The Reg Presley UFO Show* and a few years later he published a book about UFOs and phenomena called *Things They Don't Tell Us*.

★

Like I said earlier, David Bowie was the main pop star obsessed by space and UFOs when I was a kid. I didn't know this at the time, but Bowie had been into UFOs ever since he was a kid, and when he was a teenager he even co-edited a flying-saucer newsletter. In an interview with the old magazine *Creem* in the sixties he told them, 'I made sightings six, seven times a night for about a year . . . We had regular cruises that came over. We knew the 6.15 was coming in and would meet up with another one. And they would be stationary for about half an hour, and then after verifying what they'd been doing that day, they'd shoot off.'

He also gave his thoughts on how the mainstream media handled UFOs, claiming that the way they angled the stories involved so much manipulation that readers would be forced to dismiss any possibility that there was any truth behind them: 'You hit them with the various code words and they're not going to believe anything if you don't want them to'.

Like most people of his age, Bowie was bang into

Stanley Kubrick's film *2001: A Space Odyssey*, which was released in 1968 between the disaster of *Apollo 1* and the success of *Apollo 7*. Everyone was into *2001* when it came out – it was a great film. Bowie even used a twist on the title of *Space Odyssey* for his 1969 song 'Space Oddity'. I only found out during our research for this project that Bowie was partly inspired by the first colour photos of Earth from outer space when he was writing the lyrics to 'Space Oddity'. Astronaut William Anders took a photo of Earth from *Apollo 8*, in December 1968, as it came back from the dark side of the moon. Most of the newspapers printed the picture and obviously it was a big fucking deal. I was a bit too young to appreciate it fully at the time, but I can imagine now how mind-blowing it must have been. My generation onwards have all grown up seeing amazing pictures of the Earth, but imagine if you were my nana and you'd lived most of your life without really knowing what Earth, the planet that you lived on, actually looked like until one day someone goes, 'Here y'are, check this out, this is what Earth looks like in colour.'

It must have done people's heads in a bit.

Anyway, that's what Bowie's on about in 'Space Oddity' when he sings about Planet Earth being blue. He was looking at those first colour photos of Earth and imagining what it would be like to be a lone spaceman up there on your Jack Jones, just looking back at Earth.

'Space Oddity' came out just before the moon landings, and the BBC played it over footage of the moon landings. Which is a bit of an odd decision if you ask me, considering the opening lyrics are about it all going tits up in space for Major Tom. If Neil Armstrong or Buzz Aldrin's families lived in the UK at the time and were watching the BBC coverage, I bet they would have thought, 'Leave it out, mate, we're fucking worried enough about them getting back as it is!'

Bowie didn't complain though. 'Space Oddity' went on to go top five, and then it went to Number One when it was rereleased in the mid-seventies. It's still his biggest selling single in Britain. Apparently Tony Visconti refused to produce the single because he felt it was too much of a commercial gimmick. I bet he regrets that. As commercial gimmicks go, it wasn't a bad one, you know what I mean? Any band today would give it's fucking right arm for a commercial gimmick like that. I've never agreed with arguments about 'keeping it real'. It's pop music, mate. It's called pop because it's *pop*ular. The aim is to sell records. Or it used to be, before the internet.

Bowie has always been fascinated by space and space travel. One of my first clear memories of *Top of the Pops* was Bowie doing 'Starman' as Ziggy Stardust in 1972 with his electric blue guitar. Have you seen how skinny Bowie looks in that all-in-one leotard number? Fucking hell. He looks like if he turned sideways he'd disappear. But get on this, it turns out that the suit was padded. He looks like he's wasting away, the skinniest man alive, and he's wearing a fucking PADDED SUIT!

He also had another extraterrestrial single in 1973, 'Life on Mars' from *Hunky Dory*, and Major Tom cropped up again in 'Ashes to Ashes' and even a couple of decades later in 'Hello Spaceboy'.

Back in 1976 Bowie starred in *The Man Who Fell to Earth* which, even if you didn't like Bowie, was a great film. It probably had more influence on me in fashion than music at the time. Bowie had this big duffel coat and a wedged centre parting, like a mushroom centre parting. It had a big effect on what became terrace fashion.

Bowie had a huge influence on Manchester in the late seventies. When I first started going out in Manchester, there was a nightclub called Pips, which was one of our favourite hangouts. It had eleven bars spread across nine different rooms, including a Roxy Music and David Bowie room. We used to spend all our time hanging out in there because that's where all the coolest dudes hung out. A lot of the Roxy and Bowie fans would get all dressed up to go down to Pips, but we never did; we were more on the original Perry Boy vibe by then. The Perry Boys were heavily influenced by football terrace culture. In Manchester they later became known as Pure Boys and then just Boys. All that culture later led into what the press dubbed Madchester. The first time it was covered in the national press was when *i-D* magazine came up and did a piece in 1987 and called us 'Baldricks' because they reckoned we had haircuts like Baldrick from *Blackadder*. But no one in Manchester called themselves a Baldrick.

There was a story just recently about how David Bowie was offered big money to make a live comeback after his latest album, *The Next Day*, came out, but he was a bit reluctant because he was nervous about returning to the stage after so long. I remember that he once said that he originally created his alter ego, Ziggy Stardust, to deal with nerves on stage. We found this quote when we were working on this book: 'I'm not particularly a gregarious person. I had an unbearable shyness; it was much easier for me to keep on with the Ziggy thing off stage as well as on. Who was David Bowie and who was Ziggy Stardust? It was motivated by shyness.'

I'm totally with him on that. That's one of the reasons I got Bez on stage, because I never wanted to be the centre of attention. Bez was my Ziggy Stardust, in a way.

★

Cat Stevens, the singer-songwriter, was another geezer who was adamant he had an encounter, when a UFO sucked him up into the sky, back in 1973. He said, 'One night I was lying in bed and I saw this flying saucer shoot across the sky and stop over me. And it sucked me up in it. When it put me down, I shot up in bed. I know IT WASN'T A DREAM. IT WAS REAL. I KNOW it was real.'

Cat's hit song 'Longer Boats' is also about UFOs, and includes lyrics that tell you to look up in the sky in case you can see aliens looking down. Two of his other songs,

'It's a Super (Dupa) Life' and 'Freezing Steel', also include references to flying saucers. Mind you, apparently old Cat has believed a few things in his life. He's been pretty Zen, he's been into tarot cards, numerology and astrology. He's a Muslim now and goes by the name of Yusuf Islam.

While we were working on this book, we also came across the claims of Sammy Hagar, who I didn't know much about, but he was the dude who replaced David Lee Roth as lead singer in Van Halen in 1985. He never used to talk about it until he wrote his autobiography a few years ago, but then he came out with all this stuff about being abducted by aliens when he was young. In his book he describes how he had this dream where he saw a ship with two creatures inside. He felt they were connected to him, as if they were tapped into his mind through some sort of wireless connection. But then he went on MTV and said it wasn't a dream – he reckoned it had really happened to him. 'It was real. Aliens were plugged into me. It was a download situation. This was long before computers or any kind of wireless. There weren't even wireless telephones. Looking back now, it was like, "Fuck, they downloaded something into me!" Or they uploaded something from my brain, like an experiment. "See what this guy knows."'

Which is pretty far out stuff, do you know what I mean?

★

46

Loads of bands have also written songs about or referenced the Roswell incident over the years. The Pixies wrote a song about Roswell called 'Motorway to Roswell' on their *Trompe le Monde* album. I always like the Pixies. Our first big tour of the US was in 1989, supporting them. I wasn't a massive fan of their music before that tour, but I really liked them as a live band and they were a lot better than us musically at that point. I got on well with them as well, especially Kim the bass player who later joined the Breeders. Actually, it was on that same Pixies tour that I first saw David Bowie in person. The night we played in Los Angeles, we went out to this club called Enter the Dragon and the Beastie Boys were there, and then the man himself, David Bowie, walked in. Gaz Whelan, our drummer, was off his head and started going, 'Ha ha – Bowie's a midget! Bowie's a midget.' He was always obsessed by people's height for some reason. He wasn't that wild, Gaz, but we were always having to try and shut him up if he got drunk or off his head, because he always went over the top.

Megadeth, the heavy metal dudes, wrote a song called 'Hangar 18', which was the hangar at the Wright-Patterson Air Force base near Dayton, Ohio, where the alien aircraft from Roswell was apparently taken in 1947. Some reports claim that the US authorities continued to store and analyse bits of the UFO at Wright-Patterson for years. Megadeth even re-created the aliens from the Roswell clips for one of the videos to the song.

Dave Grohl from the Foo Fighters is obviously bang

into UFOs because 'Foo Fighters' was a term used by Allied aircraft pilots in the Second World War to describe UFOs or mysterious aerial phenomena seen in the skies while they were on their missions. He also put the first Foo Fighters album out on his own label called Roswell Records.

The Orb also put out an album in the early nineties called *U.F.Orb*, which had a track on it called 'Blue Room', which was named after the Blue Room, the supposed UFO-evidence holding room at Wright-Patterson Air Force base.

I also came across the pretty wild claim from Killah Priest, a rapper involved in the Wu-Tang Clan, who reckoned that, 'Black people come from space. When you look at the sky, it's black. Without the sunlight – forget it, it's black. In the beginning there was darkness.'

More recently, Robbie Williams has been quite open about the fact that he is bang into his UFOs and has talked about how he has seen one on three occasions. The first was growing up in Stoke-on-Trent as a kid, the second was at home in Beverly Hills – 'I was lying on my sun lounger outside at night. Above me was a square thing that passed over my head silently and shot off.' On another occasion, he described how 'This big ball of gold light turned up.' He called his 2006 tour 'Close Encounters' and also wrote a song called 'Arizona' about alien abduction in 2008. 'Seriously, I want to go out and investigate these things,' he said. 'I'm stopping being a pop star and I'm going to be a full-time ufologist.'

There was also a story recently that he was planning to buy an island called White Rock Island, off the coast of Los Angeles, to use as a UFO viewing base.

I wouldn't mind buying my own private island for UFO hunting.

So as you can see I'm far from the only musician who's interested in UFOs. Reading about all this stuff that the researchers for this book unearthed just got me even more fascinated. I couldn't wait to get out there and do some more research and investigating myself.

CHAPTER 4

Making History

WHEN WE SAT down and started to plan the TV show and the book, I had a pretty good idea of where I wanted to go with it. I was also made up that it was going to be on the History channel because I knew they would take it seriously, which is what I wanted.

I've always been well into my films and documentaries, but over the last few years, as I've chilled out a bit and spent more time at home with a young family, I've watched more and more. I could watch the History channel and Discovery all day. Unless I'm watching CBeebies with the kids or *Coronation Street* with Joanne, that's what you'll find me watching most of the time. So I kind of had an idea in my head of the sort of show that I wanted to make.

I was asked for a list of people I'd like to meet and

interview and the producers also came up with suggestions themselves. We did get off to a slightly false start because everyone involved had a different idea of the kind of show we were going to make. The first director they teamed me up with was a guy who had directed Louis Theroux documentaries. Now, I like a bit of Louis Theroux, I think he's an all right dude, but what he does is very *him*. There's no point Shaun Ryder trying to do a Louis Theroux because I'm not that sort of person. I haven't got that sort of dry personality, you know what I mean? Also, which is even more important to me, I didn't want to just go round taking the piss out of people. I don't see the point in that. Even though I don't mind that Louis Theroux, I think he does pick easy targets half the time and it would be a piece of piss to do that with the UFO believers. I'm pretty set in my own beliefs when it comes to UFOs, and I kind of know where I draw the line, but obviously it's the sort of subject that does attract a few crackpots and attention seekers. I didn't want to make a series which just dug up the most bonkers people that we could all have a laugh at – what, with me giving little sly looks to the camera and making snidey comments behind their backs? Nah, mate, that's exactly the show I didn't want to make.

It's a subject that I'm really interested in so I wanted to meet some serious dudes: people that I'd read about or seen interviewed over the years and had found fascinating. People who have had their own experiences and encounters, whether they're similar to mine or not.

I've been interested for years in a couple of the folks that you'll read about in this book and have always wanted to meet them. People like Travis Walton, a lumberjack from Arizona who swears he was abducted by aliens in 1975. Travis wrote a book about his experience and Hollywood even made a film about his encounter called *Fire in the Sky*, which is one of my favourite movies. I saw it when it first came out in 1993, but Travis's encounter actually happened around the same time I had my first encounter.

After I saw the film I read anything I could find about the case, but that was before the internet had taken off really, and before I got into the Discovery and History channels. Since then I've seen Travis on TV loads, but I have only ever seen him interviewed on American shows, never a British show like the one we were setting out to make. Most of the interviews I've seen are also old because Travis decided to take a step back from all publicity and television for quite a few years and not do anything. He's only recently decided to come back into the limelight a bit. So Travis was a cert for me.

I found it a bit unusual that Travis's case grabbed me so much. To be honest, I think most cases of alien abduction are bullshit. When people come out and say they've been abducted by aliens, I think you can tell pretty much every time they're talking nonsense.

Probably the most famous abduction case is the Betty and Barney Hill one. They were an American couple who claimed to have been abducted by extraterrestrials in New Hampshire in 1961. They were driving back from a holiday at Niagara Falls when they saw what they thought was a UFO, which they reckoned followed them and started playing cat-and-mouse with them. At one stage, they claimed, they saw some humanoid figures in the spaceship and one of them told them, 'Stay where you are and keep looking.' They then woke up in their car to find their clothes ripped, their watches stopped at the same time and with no memory of the previous two hours. In UFO circles this is called a 'Missing Time case'. They wrote a book about their experience called *The Interrupted Journey* and it was made into a movie in 1975 called *The UFO Incident*. No disrespect to Betty and Barney, but I'm just not having their story. I've never met them but sometimes you just get a vibe, don't you? Loads of people have bought into it, so good luck to them, but everything I've seen and read about it doesn't quite add up to me.

I've also read a lot about other abduction cases and seen documentaries on them, and most of it is just bullshit to me. Most of the abductees come across as fantasists or attention seekers. I'm just not having it.

The only one that got to me, the only one that really interested me, and the only one who I could say, hand on heart, I believe, is Travis Walton. It's not just Travis either. He was with a bunch of his co-workers at the time, and they all witnessed what happened and they have all passed several polygraph tests testifying to what they saw. There were about eight of them, who were all lumberjacks, and they just worked together – they weren't all mates.

Travis and his brother-in-law, Mike Rogers, who was in charge of them all, obviously got on, but the rest of them didn't and a few of them hated each other. They were just grafters who ended up lumped together on a job. They had no loyalty to each other or anything. You know what it's like when you're forced to spend loads of time working with people who you don't exactly see eye-to-eye with? You end up hating them. They do your head in on a daily basis. Doesn't matter if you're in the rock'n'roll game like I am, or a postie like I used to be when I had my first encounter, or you work in a dull-as-fuck Ricky Gervais-type office or you're a lumberjack like Travis . . . if a group of people are lumped together like that and they don't particularly get on, they'll end up hating each other and you get little cracks in the group. This geezer doesn't like this geezer . . . this other geezer thinks that him over there is a knob – it's the same in any line of work.

But Travis and the other lumberjacks who were there that night have all stuck to the same story for forty years. Forty years. Sometimes they've been split up and interviewed separately by experts and on TV, they've done untold polygraph tests – with different cops and specialists – and for forty years every one of them has stuck to the same story. Most of them aren't in touch with each other now, but they all still insist it happened.

If you take a bunch of normal blokes who commit a crime – rob a post office or something like that – then at least one of them will betray the others or stop sticking to the story. Trust me, I've seen it with my own eyes enough times. When you're in a band you have a bit of a party line that you stick to, but at some point it will fall apart. The party line might just be to play up to the public image that you have. We had it in Happy Mondays – we might have been naughty lads when we were younger but that image, particularly of me and Bez, becomes almost exaggerated, becomes a caricature. When anyone thinks of the Mondays, they just think we were a bunch of wreckheads, and we played along with that for a long time. But then someone in the band doesn't like that and wants to prove they're a proper, serious musician. Whenever you get a bunch of blokes together on a job, any job, over time cracks will appear and you'll start to get a different version of events.

But no matter how much they hated each other, the lumberjacks stuck to the story. One of the guys went round to Travis's house and wanted to batter him because Travis said in his account that this geezer was crying when it happened. Even though he was fucking furious with Travis for saying that, and wanted to have it out with him there in the street, he still didn't suggest that the events hadn't really happened.

So that's why Travis was one of the first people I wanted to meet.

★

I also wanted to meet scientists and experts who could give me their opinion. I love watching guys like Michio Kaku on TV. He's an American theoretical physicist who has worked on stuff like string theory. I wanted to meet some top scientific minds and see what they had to say on the matter. I didn't mind one bit if some of them disagreed with me or even dismissed my take on things – I just wanted to present a proper balanced look at the subject. I'm no Jeremy Paxman, but I also wanted to see if I could get some of those top scientists to say on camera what they're afraid of saying. I do find that some of these guys will say stuff off the record that they are frightened to say on camera, as they think people will laugh at them or it might be damaging to their career, so I was keen to find out what they really thought.

Nick Pope was also top of my list. He was employed at the Ministry of Defence and worked his way up until, in 1991, he was put in charge of their 'UFO desk'. His job was to investigate and analyse all claims of UFO sightings in this country and work out if they were a threat or not. When he got the gig, Nick was a UFO sceptic, which is probably why he got the nod in the first place. But after three years in the job, he couldn't deny that there was something in the UFO sightings, that there was definitely something there. So he left the job and has since written several books about UFOs, warning us that 'extraterrestrial spacecraft are visiting Earth and that something should be done about it urgently'.

I was a little bit wary about some of the people I was

going to meet along the way. I think sometimes you need to question the qualifications of some of the so-called 'experts' that crop up on TV. A lot of them seem to be self-proclaimed specialists, especially when it comes to a subject like UFOs. Whenever I'm watching the BBC News or Sky News, I'm always sceptical when they produce some 'specialist' or 'expert'. I know how it works. There will be a story about something random, could be anything . . . say there's a story about frogs. So whoever is the researcher on duty at the TV channel that day gets told, 'Right, we need an expert on frogs, find us one quick!' So the researcher rings round everyone they know, trying to find someone who knows something about frogs, and they find someone who might have only seen a few frogs, but he's read a bit about them as well, and he can do a quick bit of Googling before he comes on to refresh his memory. Then the newsreader goes, 'Right, now over to our frog expert Joe Smith or Shaun Ryder or whatever his name is . . .' They're only on TV for seven seconds but it's come up with a caption with their name and 'Frog Expert', so now everyone assumes they're a fucking frog expert. Next time there's some news story about frogs, all the channels will be going, 'Try and get hold of that frog expert that they used last time, what was his name, Shaun Ryder or something?' It just snowballs like that, and all of a sudden, from being a geezer who'd only seen a few frogs, he's now officially an expert, and he goes round giving talks at frog conferences, and being flown here, there and everywhere to give his opinion on bloody frogs.

That's how some of these 'experts' start out, so I always like to suss 'em out for myself. Don't ever believe someone's an expert just 'cos the telly tells you they are. Trust me. They haven't gone to university and got a doctorate in frogs – they've bumbled into it. So let's just say I wasn't going to swallow everything that the UFO experts we met told me.

I didn't want the programme to be dry, all scientists and experts, and I definitely didn't want to be only meeting a load of oddballs with outlandish claims. I was looking for something in the middle, something serious, but I also wanted to meet people who'd had similar experiences to myself.

With that mixture of people, I was pretty sure we'd find something entertaining, but also get a little closer to the truth.

CHAPTER 5

UFO Highway, Chile

THERE WERE A few reasons I decided to start my search for UFOs in Chile. One was the fact that it seems to have been a huge hotbed of activity in recent years. Chile is the UFO capital of South America. If they haven't seen one themselves, then most Chileans have someone in their family who has seen a UFO or has had some sort of encounter. The whole of South America seems to be pretty lively to me, to be honest, when it comes to stories like this. I've also seen a lot of documentaries and films about incidents that have happened right across South America, and the people there seem much more open to believing than they are back home.

I remember hearing about a supposed alien skeleton that was found in the desert in Chile that caused a bit of a stir. But then it turned out to be the mummified remains of a deformed human being. I also remember that big story in Brazil in the mid-nineties, the Varginha incident, when there were quite a few spottings of a red devil-type creature, with brown skin and red eyes, that the military had allegedly captured. I've seen loads of stuff like that on documentaries over the years, so I knew it was pretty lively in South America and it seemed a great place to kick off.

Chile has more UFO sightings per square kilometre than almost anywhere else on the planet, and the country's media is awash with reports of mysterious happenings in its skies. I'm sure this is partly because the night sky is so clear there. Ask anyone who's been to Chile and they will tell you that they've never seen so many stars in their life.

One of the things we found out before we went is that most of the observatories in the southern hemisphere are in Chile because the sky is so clear. Even the UK, the US and Japan all have interests in observatories in Chile. Part of the reason is because we've mapped the northern hemisphere now, so we might as well crack on with the southern hemisphere.

The other main reason I chose Chile for the place to start my investigations is the fact that the government are so open out there. While most governments refuse to publicize UFO sightings, Chile comes at it from the totally opposite angle. They have their own government agency called CEFAA, which made me think of Ceefax every time I heard someone say it. Ceefax was a bit of a weird invention, wasn't it? I remember when it started in the seventies and they've only just stopped it. Who the fuck was using it for the last couple of years? No one, probably. You've got to feel sorry for the people who were working on it near the end, who were probably thinking, 'Will anyone actually *ever* read this?'

In English CEFAA stands for the 'Committee for the Study of Anomalous Aerial Phenomena', and they're the bods who are in charge of investigating 'strange air phenomena' in Chile. They're also the only government agency in the world that is releasing hard physical evidence of UFOs. That was a big bonus for me. It's not often you get government officials saying, 'What's that? You want to talk about UFOs that have been spotted in our country? Sure, come down, Shaun, we'll show you everything that we've got here and talk you through the various incidents . . .' You're not going to get that kind of response in fucking America, are you? Or back home in Britain. Can you imagine tipping up at Area 51 and them saying, 'Oh, you want to know the truth about the Roswell incident? Yeah, no bother, come in, follow me, we'll show you everything that we've got here . . .'

Chile is a mad country really. It's just a massive long strip, almost 3,000 miles long, stretching down the west coast of South America, sandwiched between the Andes and the Pacific Ocean. I flew into the capital Santiago, which is half way down the country. I've been to South America a few times with the Mondays and after twenty hours on a plane it always feels like I've arrived at the edge of the world. Our first trip was quite mental – it was in January 1990 at the height of our madness. When I think back to that trip now, it seems like it happened to a different person. But then I suppose it did, because I'm now very different to the Shaun Ryder I was then. We were playing the Maracana, the huge football stadium in Rio de Janeiro where the World Cup final will be held in 2014. Not bad for your first gig in Brazil, eh? It was part of this huge 'Rock in Rio' gig. A few journalists flew with us on the plane, including James Brown from *NME*, who later went on to start *Loaded*, and Piers Morgan, who was then a reporter on the *Sun*. Piers got his baptism into life on the road with the Mondays when he sat near to PD (Paul Davis), our keyboard player, on the plane over. PD just pulled out a big bag of coke and got stuck in there and then on the plane. Just pulled a towel over his head and snorted his little head off.

We were all in first class, and when we landed in Rio all these military-type dudes in sunglasses and dark suits got on and marched down the aisle going, 'Where iz Happy Mondays?' and we were all thinking 'Fuck!' So the band and all our crew were marched off the plane. We all thought we were going to get searched and thrown in jail, but it turned out our pal who lived in Rio and was well connected had arranged for us to be swept straight through security. Which was nice.

While we were in Rio, Piers Morgan set it up for us to go round to the Great Train Robber Ronnie Biggs's house for a barbecue. He wanted to get a picture of the Mondays with the Great Train Robber for the *Sun*. That was Piers's idea of great journalism. I actually really liked Ronnie Biggs – he was a top geezer and we got on well because he was a fellow Leo. We also went to some really offside club called Help, which was a crazy night and it all got pretty hairy. We were lucky to get out alive, but I've told that full story in my autobiography, and no UFOs were involved. It was a crazy trip but I loved it, despite the hairy moments.

I've only actually been to Chile once before and that was the year before, when we'd played here with the Mondays. We did some big gig in Santiago, the capital, but we were only there for a couple of days, literally just in and out, and I hardly left my hotel room. I've never been one for exploring or sightseeing when I'm on tour with the band. When we first started touring the world with the Mondays, years ago, my idea of sightseeing was to jib off and score. But all that's behind me, a long time ago. Nowadays, I generally just prefer to chill out in my room. Touring is a young man's game really - now we get some time off in between gigs I'm quite happy chilling in my room, watching a few films or documentaries. So when we'd been here in Chile the year before, I'd hardly seen anything of Santiago, apart from what I'd seen coming in from the airport, from my hotel window or from the stage. Ask any musician and that's all they generally see on tour. I don't think many musicians spend their day off visiting cathedrals and art galleries. They're all too knackered. It takes it out of you, even when you're not partying hard.

The researchers from the History channel had done their homework before we arrived and hooked us up with some of the top UFO bods in the country, so I was keen to crack on and see what we could discover.

Shaun's X-Files

Chile is unusual in being among a number of countries that officially take UFOs seriously, so much so that in 1997 the government set up CEFAA (which is pronounced see-fa) to analyse and study all sightings of UFOs and strange air phenomena reported in the country. Once CEFAA is certain an object is truly unidentifiable, it officially releases the footage.

The agency is open about its findings and is governed by the 2008 law 20.285, known as the 'Transparency Law', designed so that government agencies act in an open and transparent manner. Most countries that have released UFO records have done so primarily in the area of government paper files but none have released hard physical evidence like Chile's CEFAA. It has released a different category of ufological evidence including photos, video and extraordinary audio recordings from pilots witnessing UFOs.

We went to pay a visit to CEFAA in Chile's Aeronautics and Space Museum in Santiago. The museum reminded me a bit of the Museum of Science and Industry in

Manchester, although it was obviously dedicated to planes and space. It was a huge old hangar space, with some mad old planes and exhibitions on space travel. CEFAA was actually based out the back, in what was, without being rude, pretty much basically just a couple of Portakabins knocked together to create a small office. I don't know what we were expecting, really. I suppose it was never going to be some huge command centre like you see on the Apollo missions or in that film *War Games*, where that kid Matthew Broderick nearly sets off World War Three by hacking into the US military computers. He'd get sent down for about 135 years if he did that in real life now. The CEFAA team were really friendly though, and welcomed the crew in and made them tea and biscuits, which was nice of them. They had a big map of Chile on the wall, with pins stuck in where there had been various UFO spottings that they were investigating.

This Chilean real life X-Files team is headed up by an ex-Air Force dude called General Ricardo Bermúdez. He and his team investigate and document any reported unidentified flying objects, and then, and this is the difference with every other country, they release their findings and make them available to the public. General Ricardo Bermúdez is a pretty friendly dude, and happy to discuss their findings face-to-face and on camera. The most important thing he says is, 'We can say that this phenomenon is present in our controlled air space and outside it as well', i.e. he thinks UFOs exist, according to all the official evidence that he's seen. So, we've only been here twenty-four hours and we've already had the head of a government department telling us, on camera, that after seeing all the evidence they had, he's sure UFOs exist. Not a bad day's work.

★

After a night's kip back at the hotel, I'm up early for my first full day proper of UFO hunting. Well, I say early, but I've got two young kids, Lulu and Pearl, so 7.30 a.m. is a lie-in for me these days. I'm usually up around sixish most days. Get up and make a cup of coffee if the kids aren't up. Probably get roped into watching some cartoon if they are. Or maybe take them for an early morning swim as we've got an indoor pool out the back of our house.

One of the main guys the production team wants me to meet while we're here is Antonio Huneeus, a renowned ufologist, who has been studying UFOs for twenty years. He's led quite a mad life, old Antonio. He's from Santiago and studied journalism at the University of Chile before moving to New York when he was still quite young in the late seventies, and he had all sorts of jobs there, but began to make a name for himself writing about UFOs. He's written a few books on UFOs and was awarded 'Ufologist of the Year' at the National UFO Conference in Miami in 1990, so he knows his shit. He's now editor and reporter for a UFO organization in the States called Open Minds, which has a website and a magazine and organizes conferences. So he's a pretty well-respected authority on UFOs. It was also good to have someone local with us anyway, as they help explain differences in culture and how locals might see things. I meet him at the hotel and we get to know each other over a coffee. Not that Antonio really needs the coffee – he's quite a hyperactive dude and he never seems to stop talking, which I could see I was going to have to get used to over the next few days.

The first incident we are off to investigate with Antonio is the case of El Bosque Air Force base. El Bosque is just outside Santiago, where something very strange happened a couple of years ago. Every four years at El Bosque they have what they call a change of guard of the Commander-in-Chief of the Chilean Air Force (FACH). They bump off the last dude (not literally) and get some new kid in to take his place. It's a pretty big deal for them so they have this whole ceremony, a big show-of-power thing, with loads of the Air Force planes doing flight passes and demonstrations at El Bosque, like the Chilean answer to the Red Arrows.

The last time they changed Commander-in-Chief and had this big parade was in 2010, when the current dude, who's called General Jorge Rojas Ávila, became the new chief, and the big all-singing, all-dancing, all-flying ceremony took place in El Bosque in the morning of 1 November. Everything on the day seemed to go according to plan and nobody noticed anything unusual during the ceremony.

So far, so pretty dull. But this is where it gets interesting.

Although no one noticed anything on the day, when these military dudes and their families went home and started watching the footage they'd shot on their video cameras or mobiles or whatever, a few of them spotted something very weird on their footage. Antonio shows me the footage on his iPad. It's pretty crazy. This unidentified object, whatever it is, shoots across the sky in broad daylight, just behind the jet fighters that are in formation. I think the fact that it's moving so bloody quick is probably one of the main reasons why no one on the ground really spotted it at the time. When they watched the footage they were like, 'Hang on, what the fuck is that?' They weren't UFO spotters or anything, they were just normal Chilean Air Force cadets and engineers who were there.

You can't see it with the naked eye because it's moving so fast – it's only when you slow it down you can see what looks like a tiny craft shooting across the sky during the ceremony. Seven different dudes caught the same thing on camera that day, and all their different footage shows this small, dome-shaped, flat-bottomed metallic object zooming across the sky. It's buzzing around the fighter planes in the Air Force display and moving much, much faster than them. Antonio says that none of the pilots on the day noticed anything unusual. I ask Antonio what speed he reckons the unidentified object was doing.

Antonio tells me about the top scientists and military specialists who have seen the footage. 'One of the rough estimates was eighteen times the speed of the planes. One of the great things about this footage is they know the speed of the planes, so they can judge the speed of the [unidentified flying] object against the planes, and also you can judge the size and speed of it against the mountains. Usually, footage is in the dark, so you have nothing to judge it against. Here we have known parameters to measure it against which we don't normally have.'

I know what he means as half the footage you see of what people think is a UFO just looks like a blob in the sky, and there's no way of judging how big it is – it could be an insect or it could be a craft the size of the Starship *Enterprise*.

Antonio explains how there have been numerous cases of pilots reporting weird flying objects over the years, but virtually no footage like this where the unidentified flying object has been caught on film at the same time as terrestrial planes.

If you ask me, after looking at the footage again, something that size, that is moving eighteen times faster than fighter jets, is definitely not from this planet.

CEFAA was contacted by these seven different people individually after they'd all been freaked out by their footage. A number of CEFAA experts have studied these recordings and the agency has confirmed this as an unidentified object travelling at speeds in excess of 4,000 mph. The footage was eventually released to the public in March 2012, but no explanation has been found.

At the 2012 International UFO Congress, General Bermúdez, the big cheese of CEFAA, said that after analysis by all their astronomers, Air Force specialists and internal military personnel, 'it has been confirmed that the UFO captured in the footage is an unknown aerial phenomenon'. This obviously caused a bit of a stir in the global UFO community and, as you'd expect, loads of them jumped on it as the solid evidence of UFOs they've been waiting for.

The production team has arranged for us to go to the Air Force base and see exactly where this happened, and meet some of the witnesses, which is exciting. Me and Antonio jump in a people carrier and set off through Santiago. The traffic is a nightmare and the smog is also pretty terrible. It reminds me a bit of Los Angeles, the way it settles over the downtown area. I tell Antonio this and have a bit of a chat with him about the similarities between Santiago and LA. 'Well, you know the climate is similar,' he says, 'and the smog comes down from the mountains in Santiago and settles over downtown in a similar way to the way it does in Los Angeles. Also, Chile and Los Angeles are both famous for their wine, and they also both have quite a bit of a new age culture.' That's a bit of LA I could never be arsed with, I tell him, all that new age bollocks.

'Of course, both California and Chile are also good spots for UFOs.'

Which is why I'm here, obviously. I decide to pick Antonio's brains about why he thinks people are obsessed by UFOs.

'Even the sceptics have to recognize that, at least as a

sociological phenomenon, UFOs are real, in other words, people see stuff. No one can deny that. But we don't know what it is, which is why we call them UFOs.'

I tell Antonio about my second encounter, when I saw a UFO on the way to work as a postman early one morning, and he's really interested and tells me that his first sighting was pretty similar. He was in Santiago in 1988: 'I saw lights, it looked like a star, but it was moving like crazy, and then it would stop, and it went on for like twenty minutes or something.'

Apparently this type of sighting is pretty common. Two-thirds of all close encounters of the first kind, i.e. sightings of UFOs, are pretty similar to mine and Antonio's – mysterious lights in the night sky, moving at very unusual speeds and performing mad, fast changes of direction that would be impossible for any plane that we've invented.

I also tell Antonio about my first sighting, when I looked up in the sky and saw literally hundreds of small lights, and my belief that there is life out there. He agrees with me: 'I mean, the universe is so huge why would there just be one place with life? It doesn't make sense.'

I also tell him that I think if the authorities announced tomorrow that we've made contact with an alien race then a lot of people would go bananas. What's mad is that Antonio then starts telling me about a famous Arthur C. Clarke TV series in the eighties that he loved called *Arthur C. Clarke's Mysterious World*, which I actually remember watching as an eighteen-year-old on Granada TV. Pretty crazy to go to the other side of the world and find a local banging on about something that you saw on local TV when you were growing up.

Arthur C. Clarke's Mysterious World was a thirteen-part series that looked at 'unexplained phenomena from around the world' and one of the episodes was all about UFOs. They looked at the Robert Taylor incident, which happened in Scotland in 1979 and is also called the Livingston incident or the Dechmont Woods encounter. Old Bob Taylor was a forester (a bit like Travis Walton) who reported seeing an extraterrestrial spacecraft. His was the first UFO case that was officially investigated by the Scottish dibble. I think it's still the only UFO sighting in the UK that has been the subject of a criminal investigation. They also looked at the case of Kenneth Arnold, who was an American dude who made what is considered to be the first report of seeing a UFO in the US, in 1947.

Antonio also gives me a copy of a book that he helped research called *Alien Rock – The Rock'n'roll Extraterrestrial Connection*, by Michael C. Luckman, who is the director of the New York Center for Extraterrestrial Research and the founder of the Cosmic Majority, 'an organization of people on Earth who believe in UFOs, life on Mars, and the paranormal'. Antonio shows me a passage in the book which talks about how a bunch of Chilean musicians including Tito Fernández, Jorge Cruz and Gloria Benavides had a mad experience when they were on tour in northern Chile in 1974. They were driving through a remote part of the desert called Pampa Soledad, which means 'pampa of solitude', when they spotted a light, which then began to chase them. They were convinced it was a UFO and it ended up chasing them for nearly an hour, with one of the musician dudes hanging out of the window of their car, waving a crucifix at the UFO to try and ward it off. As if that wasn't weird enough, the orange light then split in half, like an orange into two segments, and they could see a tall humanoid figure about seven feet tall appear. Needless to say, they all shit themselves and raced to the nearest cop station, but when they got there the UFO had disappeared. Seventeen years later, in 1991, another group of people had a very similar episode on the same stretch of road in the Pampa Soledad, although this time it was a green light and they managed to catch a bit of it on a camcorder. Very strange.

Shaun's X-Files

To put the mathematical chance of life elsewhere in the Universe into perspective, you need to understand Earth's place within it. Our galaxy contains an estimated 400 billion stars – if only 0.001 per cent of these have some kind of life, that still leaves forty million planets that could support life. Then if you consider that our galaxy is just one of billions in the known universe, it's enough to twist anyone's melon.

It takes us about an hour to get to the El Bosque Air Force base on the outskirts of Santiago. When we get there, I can't believe how easy it is to get in, considering how important this base is. I mean, I know they're expecting us, but even so, we just tip up at the front gate and they let us straight through. No checking of ID or passports, no searches, no checking the vehicle or anything. Piece of piss. Getting into Disneyland is harder than that. I'm not joking. I once did a gig there with Happy Mondays about ten years ago and it was a fucking nightmare. They have Mickey Mouse security there. I'm not taking the piss, the security there actually did have badges that say 'Mickey Mouse security', but they were anything but Mickey Mouse. They were actually really on top. If you've ever been to Disneyland you will know they have venues, nightclubs, Hard Rock Cafes and all sorts in there, and we were playing one of the venues. It was a nightmare trying to get to the venue with the band and all our gear, past all the security, and once we were there they didn't want us to move. We couldn't go anywhere. They just wanted us to stay backstage until we went on – we couldn't even jib off for a little look around Disneyland or anything, not that I would have wanted to. It would look a bit weird, a few forty-year-old men mooching around Disneyland on their own, you know what I mean? I'd take my kids there, but it's not the sort of place you go with your pals unless you want a few weird looks.

Anyway, it's smooth as anything getting into El

Bosque and when we get inside, Commander Perry, one of their top fighter pilots and instructors, is waiting for us. It feels a bit like the Tom Cruise film *Top Gun*. All the pilots are wearing those all-in-one jumpsuits that you sometimes see trendy dicks in East London wearing. Commander Perry is obviously top boy here – he is a pretty relaxed dude but you can tell everyone respects him. He reminds me of the main instructor with the 'tache in *Top Gun*. He shows us around the gaff a bit, and explains what they get up to, how the skies here are full of planes every day, but how they had never had an incident like the one that happened that day in 2010.

Commander Perry was actually flying himself during the event and describes the day to me. He says he was flying 'about 350 knots an hour'. I thought knots were how they measured how fast boats were travelling, not planes, but anyway, that's about the same as 400 miles an hour. Now that means if this object was travelling at eighteen times the speed of the planes, it was going at least 7,000 miles an hour.

CEFAA have a pretty rigorous way of looking through all the videos and information they receive. They don't just sit there watching clips and going, 'Wow, check this out!' They have all sorts of tests, and 95 per cent of the stuff they receive they clarify in some way or just discard. They either work out what it is and have a logical explanation for it, or they can tell it's bollocks. It's the other 5 per cent that interests them. And me.

Of the seven videos captured that day, so far only one has been officially released by CEFAA. In it the suspicious object passes through the frame several times as military jets take part in the air show.

Commander Perry takes me to the exact spot where the video was shot, and it's easy to recognize it from the video. He repeats that neither he nor the other pilots saw anything unusual on the day, but he's obviously fascinated by what showed up on the film. I ask him what he thinks it is, and he says: 'It's nothing military or civilian . . . it's not a bird . . . so maybe it is not of this planet.'

He seems a pretty stand-up dude and he's obviously well-respected in the Air Force, so it's good to hear that coming from him. He then tells me about another film from that day that they've only just discovered, which is music to my ears. It was shot by one of the Air Force guys, but he's only just realized that he caught the UFO on there. Not only has it never been seen in public before, even CEFAA don't know it exists.

We all pile into the base's command centre, and they show us the footage on a big screen. Commander Perry talks us through it. There's only a brief glimpse of the object on the film, but I'm sure it's the same UFO as the one on the original El Bosque video. It's more than I expected to find on my first proper day UFO hunting in Chile, and I'm pretty blown away by how helpful everyone has been. You'd never get this reception at a military base back home. Commander Perry even arranges for me to get a copy of the footage to take away

with me. My first day and I've come away with some
UFO footage that even the government hasn't seen yet.
It bodes pretty well for the rest of my trip.

CHAPTER 6

The Andes and the Stormtroopers

THE NEXT MORNING, we're heading east out of Santiago to a place called Cajón del Maipo, which is one of Chile's UFO *zonas calientes* or 'hot zones'. It's a pretty beautiful area – there's a huge canyon at the bottom of the Andes, with various rivers running through it, so there's a lot of trekking and rock climbing, and it's always been big with tourists from home and abroad. But a lot of the locals are convinced that there are also visitors coming here from much further afield – other star systems – which is why I'm off to take a look for myself.

Cajón del Maipo is a bit like the Lake District, but more extreme. Not long after we got out of Santiago the scenery changed and became a lot greener, much greener than I'd expect Chile to be. Then as we start climbing higher it gets rockier. The landscape seems to change every fifteen minutes. It's still beautiful though, with ravines, rivers and all sorts. We are in two 4 × 4s with two local drivers, Pancho (who is also one of our cameramen) and Jorge, and they tell me how it's an amazing place for rock climbing, which they are both bang into. Pancho travels all over the world to do his climbing, and shows us some pictures of some of the crazy cliffs and rocks he's climbed in Arizona and other places. He even takes part in climbs that take over twenty-four hours, when he has to sleep in one of those tents that you just hang off the side of a cliff. Mad bastard. His mate Jorge also used to work here in Cajón del Maipo, looking after part of the land, so he knows it very well. In my experience a lot of people who are into extreme sports can often be dicks, but Pancho and Jorge are cool dudes, and it's good to have them on board.

Shaun's X-Files
The Andes is the longest mountain range in the world, stretching 4,300 miles through seven countries. Formed 138 million years ago when the South American and Nazca tectonic plates smashed together, they rise to a height of almost 7,000 metres and are home to scenery as brutal as it is beautiful. Not only that, they play host to some of the clearest skies anywhere on the planet – perfect for spotting any extraterrestrial visitors.

We are heading to San José de Maipo, a small town high up in the valley, where the production team has arranged for me to meet ufologist Miguel Jordan. He's been coming here looking for UFOs since the early nineties and he's had a few experiences himself, so I am keen to see what he has in store for me. I meet him in the town square and I can tell straightaway that he takes the business of UFOs pretty seriously. He knows the area well and explains to me that more than 40 per cent of the locals in the area have seen UFOs. Which seems pretty high to me. We decide to get chatting to a few of the locals in the town square and find out if many of them have had personal encounters, and then after that drive further up in the mountains to spend the night UFO watching.

In 2002, the Mayor of San José de Maipo declared it a UFO-tourism zone after he and so many other locals made sightings – although I suppose a cynic might say that's just a way to build tourism, isn't it?

It was a pretty sunny afternoon and there were people sat around the square on benches and people having a bite to eat, so I thought I'd go and test out what Miguel's been saying about the high number of sightings.

Miguel is pretty confident but the first family hasn't seen one, so we move on. The second guy we speak to is an old fella who worked for forty-three years in a hydroelectric power station up in the hills nearby. Forty-three years! You get less for murder. The old dude reckons that UFOs were '*always* showing up there'. He says his colleagues saw them as well, many times over the years, and he describes them as moving lights, similar to what I saw when I had my first encounter. I can't speak Spanish for toffee, but when me and the old guy are explaining our encounters to each other, we almost don't need Miguel to translate. We're on the same wavelength.

Everyone that we speak to in the square seems pretty friendly, even those who are not interested in UFOs or don't want to be on camera. If I tried the same thing with a camera crew wandering down Deansgate in Manchester, asking people if they had seen a UFO, I'd get some pretty strange reactions from people. I wonder if the openness here is down to what they've witnessed or something more fundamental.

After a while Miguel is mega keen to get on the road for the night's UFO watching. He explains we must set off a few hours before sunset in order to make sure that we find a remote spot away from all light sources, ready for a night of skywatching. He tells me he wants to be sure that if we see a UFO there is no confusing it with light from human sources. He also tells me it's going to be pretty fucking nippy up there, as we're going up to the snowline, and as we'll be up there most of the night we need warm clothing, torches and all sorts of other supplies. He takes himself pretty seriously, old Miguel.

As we drive up there Miguel explains, in his quite serious way that I'm getting used to by now, that although we might want to see a UFO tonight, our best hope is to only see one at a distance because a close encounter would not be nice. I'm not quite sure what he's on about. If you can see a UFO, then technically, that *is* a close encounter. For someone who is a ufologist, he seems really pretty uncomfortable with the idea of actually coming into contact with a UFO, almost as if he's frightened of them, but that fear is like a drug that he feeds off.

We drive further up into the canyon, up the rocky mountain roads, and I can see why we needed a 4 × 4 to get up here. There are boulders and huge potholes in the road that we have to dodge round. I've got a Range Rover back home in Salford, but I wouldn't fancy bringing it up here.

We get further and further away from civilization until we find ourselves in the flat bottom of a canyon with snowy peaks all around us. This is the location Miguel recommends for tonight. It's a pretty incredible spot. There's no one else around and we feel a bit small in the bottom of this huge canyon. Even the big 4 × 4s look like Matchbox cars against the looming mountains. It's almost dark by the time we arrive and bloody freezing; it's hard to believe that we were in the sunny square in San José de Maipo only a couple of hours ago.

When I get out and look up at the sky, though, it's unbelievable. I've gazed at the sky all my life, but I've never seen a sky like this. Like I said at the start of the book, one of my earliest memories as a little kid is lying on the top bunk bed in the bedroom that I shared with Our Paul and just gazing up at the sky. I've done it ever since. I still do it now. My clubbing days are over, so if I'm not away working and I'm at home, you'll often find me out in the back garden at night, staring up at the sky. I've been round the world numerous times on tour and seen a million night skies, but I've never seen anything like the sky here in Chile tonight (although when you're on tour with a rock'n'roll band you're mostly staying in big cities). I've never seen so many stars.

The sky is so clear that you can understand why there have been so many reported sightings of UFOs around this part of Chile. Within about the first ten minutes I see one of the most amazing shooting stars I've ever seen. It's pretty obvious that if there is anything unusual in the sky around here you're going to get a good look at it. After the amount of people we've met today who have had an encounter, it's hard to believe we won't see something for ourselves as the night starts to draw in. Wayne, the director, has me on an infrared camera so he can capture my reaction to anything.

I chat to Miguel about Chile's history with UFOs. According to him, Chile has been visited by aliens for centuries. He subscribes to the theory that contact goes back far beyond the arrival of the Conquistadors and into antiquity – a hypothesis known as paleo-contact. The people who believe in that idea reckon that primitive man's exposure to ancient aliens influenced the development of culture and religion on Earth. Some of them reckon that the gods worshipped in modern-day faiths were in fact originally extraterrestrial. I'm not quite sure I'm with him on that, to be honest.

He also explains a different, interesting theory on why

aliens might want to visit Chile – the idea is that it is being used as some sort of intergalactic filling station because there are minerals or fuels here that aliens might be interested in or need.

By this time we're three hours into our night skywatch and there's been no sign of life in the dark skies above. I'm freezing my bloody nuts off, but fortunately Jorge, one of our drivers, has brought a good supply of a Chilean herbal tea, so that warms me up a bit.

Miguel seems to be a bit on edge and all of a sudden he points up into the sky and whispers urgently, 'There! There's one . . .'

'Yeah, yeah . . . I saw something,' I reply.

There is some sort of weird light in the sky where Miguel is pointing, but it's soon obvious that whatever the light is, unfortunately it's not what we're looking for. I'm starting to get the feeling Miguel is even more desperate to see a UFO than I am. Being out here at night seems to have put him on edge and, as we talk, he opens up about a UFO encounter he had a few years ago that had a deeply profound effect on him . . .

'I was a UFO researcher until 2003, well, I'm still a UFO researcher, but I haven't done so much skywatching since an incident I had in 2003. I was with another twelve or thirteen people and I had an incident of missing time.'

'Missing time' is a regular feature of UFO encounters when people realize that they are missing an hour or two or three or more, and they can't account for it.

'From that time, I don't take people to skywatch,' says Miguel, 'because I feel responsible for what happens.'

Poor Miguel seemed to be going under a bit.

'We had one or two hours' missing time,' explains Miguel. 'Most of us could not remember what happened, which is a problem. You ask yourself "What happened there?" The questions remain and you think "Maybe I will remember one day in the future." There is a risk you take when you enter into this phenomena research. But if you are a researcher you are obligated to. For me this is not a job. But I feel responsible for things that could happen to people who are with me.'

It's now the middle of the night and it's freezing. Wayne the director tells us that he once made a film about Eskimos and had to live with them for months. He would sleep in clothes made of reindeer skins at night, because that's the warmest thing you can wear, even warmer than the latest mountaineering gear. He also says they had to eat reindeer every night. I'm not sure I'd be up for that.

It is proper brass monkeys now. I feel like I have no testicles. So I decide to call it a night. It might be a UFO hotspot, but I'm just not feeling the vibe tonight. I don't think we're going to see anything. Yet, even though the night might not be lit up with alien spacecraft, standing gazing at the southern skies up here in the Andes still feels like a real privilege . . .

Miguel gets even more desperate when we say we're off home . . . we're miles from anywhere and we've got at least a three-hour drive back to Santiago, through the night, before we can finally get some shuteye. The whole crew has accepted that we aren't going to see anything tonight, but Miguel still seems on edge. Maybe he's always like this or maybe he feels responsible because he is here as the expert UFO hunter and we haven't seen anything, I don't know, but it's not as if you can wish a UFO into existence, is it? Either there is something there in the sky the night you're out there or there isn't, and all of us accepted that there wasn't anything there apart from Miguel.

★

Shaun's X-Files
On 31 January 1998 people all over Santiago observed several humanoid figures descending from the sky to hover above the city. The figures seemed to come down like paratroopers would before opening their parachutes, but then some floated in the same position, some moved in a horizontal direction and some even moved back upwards. None of the figures opened a parachute to stop their fall, but their movements defied gravity. Captured on video by various witnesses, the case caught the imagination of the country and to this day it remains unexplained.

Back in Santiago the next morning, we are off to

investigate one of Chile's most bizarre UFO incidents, which happened in the skies over the capital itself on 31 January 1998.

I'd arranged to meet Rodrigo Fuenzalida, director of Chile's leading civilian UFO group, AION, who had agreed to take me to one of the key locations relating to the incident, on the outskirts of Santiago, and talk me through the footage. Rodrigo looks a bit like a Chilean ufologist's answer to Indiana Jones. He has an Indiana Jones–type hat and a kind of safari jacket, and he takes himself quite seriously. We are following Rodrigo in his jeep and he has trouble finding the place at first, which wasn't promising. When we get there, he points in the sky to where the incident happened and then starts showing me footage on his laptop, but I can't see a thing, so we go back to his motor, out of the sun, and watch it in there. When I can see it, I can't believe my eyes. It's bonkers. One of the strangest, most mysterious things I've ever seen in my life.

The best way I can describe it is like a *Star Wars* stormtrooper, stood on a pogo stick, under a woman's hairdryer, descending out of the sky. I know that sounds crazy, but that's exactly what it looks like to me. It must have been absolutely mental to have seen it with your own eyes when it happened.

I watch it again and again with Rodrigo, and every time I watch it, it just seems even more unexplainable. 'It really does look like they're dressed in *Star Wars* gear, like a *Star Wars* stormtrooper,' I tell Rodrigo, and he laughs and agrees.

'Yes, *Star Wars* in Chile!'

'Can you imagine being stood here,' I ask him, 'and seeing this thing coming down out of the sky looking like a *Star Wars* stormtrooper on a pogo stick? It must have looked like Darth Vader was going to come down out of the sky.'

I really haven't seen anything like it before in my life. We've all seen plenty of pics and footage of UFOs, or alleged UFOs, but I've never seen anything remotely like this stormtrooper tackle. It reminds me a bit of the opening ceremony of the Olympics in Los Angeles in 1984, when that dude in a spaceship and a jet pack flew into the stadium. Every kid who watched that thought they would have one by the time they grew up but it never happened, did it? Bit like those hoverboards from *Back to the Future II* – where are they? It was 2015 in the film when all the kids were knocking about on hoverboards, so presumably they'll be about in time for next Christmas.

One of the reasons this case is unusual is the sheer number of witnesses, and their accounts are intriguing. Some motorists reported seeing some of the figures vanishing into the clouds, whilst those on the ground described other figures disappearing down into the city, never to be seen again. All very mysterious.

It's a very famous case in Chile and Rodrigo said there was a public poll done, and 70 per cent of the Chileans thought that whatever was captured on camera was extraterrestrial.

Me listening to another UFO expert. My UFO journey was one of the weirdest trips I've ever been on.

Santiago, where I started the Chile leg of my UFO trip.

General Ricardo Bermúdez, head of CEFAA, Chile's official UFO agency, set up by the government in 1998.

UFO expert and journalist Antonio Huneeus, me and Squadron Commander Perry at El Bosque Air Force base, where a unidentified flying object was captured on film, flying eighteen times faster than air force planes.

Me in Cajon del Maipo, Chile, on the edge of the Andes.

I spent all night skywatching in Cajon del Maipo, Chile, where the night sky was amazing, but we didn't see any UFOs.

Rodrigo Fuenzalida, director of Chile's leading civilian UFO group, AION.

Me in Chile's Atacama Desert, the driest desert in the world.

Me, with the Atacama Giant in the distance.

UFO expert and journalist Antonio Huneeus, astronautics researcher Nicolás Berasain and me, climbing the Atacama Giant in the desert.

Author Patricio Abusleme Hoffman, me and Humberto Rojas round the campfire in the desert.

Me and Travis Walton. Travis' story of being abducted by aliens for five days in 1975 was made into a Hollywood film called *Fire in the Sky*.

Travis and me with the Devereaux family, who had a missing time encounter.

Larry Warren, me and Travis. Larry was witness to Rendlesham, the UK's Roswell.

Me, Alan Godfrey and Travis Walton. Alan had two encounters when he was a policeman in Todmorden in the late 70s.

Me and astrobiologist Lewis Dartnall. As well as people who had witnessed incidents, I was keen to meet with scientists and academics on my UFO trip, to get their opinion.

We later checked with CEFAA, and Eugenio Ford, the guy there who was in charge of looking into the case for the government, said he eventually came to the conclusion that 'They were UFOs; unidentified flying objects.'

Shaun's X-Files

There are other similar cases to this in Chile, but they are just the tip of this very weird iceberg – this is a truly global phenomenon. There're plenty of reports on the internet of strange humanoid figures descending from the sky. In the last ten years alone sightings have been made in Mexico, India and the USA, to name but a few. Some reports *are* more credible than others, but the Santiago case is right at the top of the peculiar pile . . .

Of all of the things I've seen so far in Chile, this case is perhaps the most baffling. I know what it looks like to me, but it just defies conventional explanation. It's a mad one.

I do feel reassured, though, that Chile has been the perfect place to come and begin my search.

CHAPTER 7

Giant Alien in the Desert

ON OUR THIRD day in Chile we are off to the Atacama Desert, which is the driest desert in the world. We are headed right to the north of Chile, so we have to fly up there. We had to get up at bloody 4.30 a.m. to get to the airport, which was a bit rough. The flight is at 7.30 a.m. so it seems a bit excessive to have to check in three hours before an internal flight, but when you're filming you've got all the cameras and sound equipment and stuff so you have to check in early. We'd never do that on tour. The crew would go on ahead of us with all the gear, and then the band would arrive later.

We are flying with Sky Airlines, one of the Chilean airlines, but nothing to do with Sky TV or Rupert Murdoch. It is a pretty small plane, and the guy in a suit in front of me puts his seat right back as soon as we take

off, and he might as well have been sitting on my knee.
I hate people like that. They give us a bit of a comedy
breakfast, this bit of square omelette, but it actually tastes
all right.

We land in Iquique and as soon as we walk out of
the airport we are besieged by a scrum of locals offering
us taxis. I've never seen a taxi scrum quite so on top.
It's much worse than when we landed at Santiago. It's
like the old footage you see of the Beatles arriving at an
airport. As soon as we get through the scrum and I step
outside for a snout, the heat hits me. It isn't necessarily
that much hotter than Santiago, but because it's so dry
the heat is much more intense. The airport is literally
surrounded by desert on three sides and the ocean on
one. You step out of the door of arrivals and it's just sand,
leading up to the mountain that overlooks the airport.

We hire a 4 × 4 and set off into town. It's a half-hour
drive along the coast, but a pretty desolate drive, just sand
and mountains on the right and the ocean on the left,
with the odd shack and the occasional little shrine, which
the driver says are for people who have died. We check
into the hotel, which is right on the seafront in Iquique.
Only problem is there's a sign outside the hotel that
says 'Warning – tsunami area'. Now I'm no expert on
tsunamis, but our hotel is only three storeys high, which
I'm not sure would give you much protection from a
tsunami. At least I'm on the third floor.

The first thing we are off to investigate in the desert is a
geoglyph called the Atacama Giant. A geoglyph is a large

design on the ground, which can be made from stones or sometimes carved into the earth. The most famous ones in the world are the Nazca Lines in Peru, but we also have some back home, including a few ones of white horses or men with big dicks on the sides of hills. Some people believe some geoglyphs were made by aliens – I'm not sure I believe that, but they're definitely a weird phenomenon. Even though I'm fascinated by things like geoglyphs, I don't put it all down to weird phenomena . . . sometimes I think we just really underestimate how intelligent people were years ago. We tend to think that until quite recent times people were pretty Neanderthal and not capable of thinking outside the box or further than their next meal or their next fuck. I don't underestimate people like that.

There are more geoglyphs in the Atacama Desert than anywhere else in the world – more than 5,000. Most of them are of animals and humans, but the most famous one, the Atacama Giant, is a massive humanoid, alien-type figure, and that's the one we're off to check out.

We've arranged to meet up with a geezer called Nicolás Berasain at the hotel. He's an astronautics researcher, the founder of Exopolitics Chile, which looks at the possibility of extraterrestrial life, and a bit of a self-styled expert on the Atacama Giant. He's going to come with us to see the Giant and share his theories on it. Apparently it's a fair old drive through the desert to get to the Giant, about four hours.

Iquique is a pretty small town and within ten minutes

of setting off, the road is climbing up the steep mountainside over the town, towards the desert. It's so steep
that there are loads of crazy dudes jumping off the top
and just paragliding straight over the town and landing
in the sea, which is pretty mad to watch. Reminds me of
when Tony Wilson tried paragliding for *Granada Reports*
back in the seventies, although these dudes know what
they're doing.

We stop off briefly on the way to the Giant to have a
butcher's at a ghost town called Humberstone. They used
to mine a lot of sodium nitrate here a hundred years ago,
what they called 'white gold'. Even though it's in the
middle of the driest desert in the world, Humberstone
had its own swimming pool converted from the hull of
a ship, an opera house and everything. Then someone
in Europe invented a synthetic nitrate so no one was
arsed about buying it from Humberstone or the other
Atacama mines any more, and they closed the town
almost overnight in the 1950s. The town has just lain
deserted ever since, for sixty years, and it's pretty spooky,
as you'd imagine.

After that we head on across the desert. I've never been
in a proper desert like this before, just miles and miles of
nothingness as far as you can see. The closest I've been is
when I went to stay up in the Rif Mountains in northern
Morocco, after the Mondays split for the first time and
before I started Black Grape. I was with the singer
Donovan's daughter at the time, Oriole, and her family
had links with Bachir Attar and the Master Musicians

of Jajouka. Donovan's wife Linda had previously had a kid with Brian Jones from the Rolling Stones, and he'd recorded an album called *Brian Jones Presents the Pipes of Pan at Joujouka* with Bachir's father, Hadj Abdesalam Attar, in 1968, when he was leader of the Master Musicians of Jajouka. We got properly looked after when we went there – Bachir even sent his Mercedes to pick us up from Marrakech. It was proper bandit country, though. We were stopped on the way by the Army and police on the roadblocks, who took all our details, just in case we didn't come back. We stayed in Bachir's house, which was a sort of complex with high walls, a bit like the gaff where they eventually found Osama bin Laden. We stayed there for three weeks in the end. It was great. We just got stoned and listened to music, and made a little bit of music with them.

That's where all the hash in Morocco is grown anyway. It reminded me of *The Man Who Would Be King*, that film starring Michael Caine and Sean Connery as two rogue officers who set off from British India in search of adventure and end up becoming kings of Kafiristan.

Anyway, that trip to Morocco was the closest I've been to proper desert before, but the Atacama Desert is a different ball game. This is proper desert, no messing. There aren't many signs of life anywhere – it's a pretty alien place, just miles and miles of nothing but arid dust and rocks – and in a weird way it makes you feel like there's more chance of finding signs of extraterrestrial life than human life out here.

Like I said earlier, the Atacama Desert is the driest desert in the world and, according to experts who measure this sort of thing, there're parts of the desert where it has never rained since records began. Never. Bit different to bloody Manchester. I think there are parts of Manchester where it has never ever stopped raining since records began!

On the way, our old friend Antonio Huneeus shows us some pics of the Giant and other geoglyphs on his iPad and, as always, gives me his opinion. People have different theories on different geoglyphs – some folk think that some of them are a kind of homage to aliens, and some reckon they were made by people who had out-of-body experiences and that's why they were able to construct something that looks in proportion from the sky. The Atacama Giant is nearly 100 metres long and is the largest humanoid-like ancient geoglyph in the world. Experts reckon it was constructed between AD 800 and 1400, but probably around AD 900. Some people think it's a pre-Incan shaman holding a medicine bag and an arrow, other people think it's an ancient alien astronaut. Nicolás, our resident Giant expert, doesn't say much, probably struggling to get a word in edgeways the way old Antonio goes on with himself. He does know his shit old Antonio, I'll give him that, but he doesn't half go on.

What Nicolás does manage to squeeze in, probably when Antonio is taking a breath, is that he sides with the camp that believes the Giant is actually an ancient alien astronaut.

Shaun's X-Files

Peru's Nazca Lines may be the most famous, but geoglyphs are a truly global phenomenon. From the Australian outback to the Mojave Desert, from the Amazon rainforest to the rolling hills of middle England, no two of these curious figures are identical. Many of them are easily explained; others have more enigmatic origins.

Of the 5,000 or so geoglyphs strewn across this barren corner of northern Chile, the Atacama Giant is by far both the most impressive and mysterious. In fact, it's the largest ancient geoglyph figure in the world – almost 100 feet taller than the Statue of Liberty in New York. From ancient deity to astronomical calendar, there are several theories surrounding the meaning of this geoglyph. Some academics believe the giant was an ancient calendar for predicting where the moon would set, others think the figure's strange appearance – that of a humanoid robot-like figure – suggests it's a depiction of an alien, worshipped as a god called Tunupa by the Andean people of the time.

When we get to the Giant, it turns out it's in the middle of nowhere. As I suppose everything is in the middle of a desert. In Britain, the Giant would be a National Trust site and you wouldn't be able to get within half a mile of it. But when we arrive at the Giant, there is no one about, and certainly no one official-looking. At first sight I am a little disappointed, after everyone had been bigging it up so much. I can't deny it. I'm a bit like, 'Er, is that it?'

The Giant is up on a rocky hill called Cerro Unita, so we have to park quite far away. Maybe it's deceptive from where we park, but it doesn't look that big at all. It looks pretty fascinating, but it certainly doesn't look taller than the Statue of Liberty. Maybe they meant that small model of the statue that they've got in Las Vegas! Nicolás, our resident Giant expert, reassures us that it's longer than a football field. My manager Warren used to be a professional footballer, so he's got a good idea how long a football pitch is, and he's having none of it. It looks like the very first Space Invaders, you know, the really blocky computer characters that you got back in the day.

We set off on foot up the rocky Cerro Unita to the Giant, and obviously it does get bigger when you get closer, but it also weirdly disappears. It was created to be viewed from afar so when you get up close you can't really work out which bit is which. We reach the feet first, obviously, but then as we work our way up the mountain, we lose track of which bit goes where – we can't work out the Giant's arse from his elbow at first. Then we reach the top and we can't find the head. The outlines of the figure are only about a foot high, if that, and the whole mountainside is covered with rocks so we get a bit lost. Still, considering I've got two experts with me, one of whom is supposed to have been studying this for fifteen years, you'd think they'd be able to find the head of this Giant between them. I seem to have more idea what's what than them at times. At one stage I wonder whether everyone is just blagging me and Wayne the director has worded them up to send me on a wild goose chase. Eventually, though, we do work out where the head is.

What is crazy is how these rocks have managed to stay here for well over a thousand years even though, when you're up close, you can see it's just a few stones piled up on each other. You could easily walk up to touch or even move all these rocks as well as there's no one else around. I could rearrange them to read 'MUFC' if I wanted to. In fact, come to think of it, the Giant does look a bit like a kid's drawing of a Man United Red Devil. I pretend to take one of the rocks from the Giant's eyeballs for the camera, saying, 'This is coming back to Manchester with me!' but I'm only messing about. Believe me, though, if that Giant was in Manchester it wouldn't last until the end of the day, let alone a thousand years. Some scally would have had its eyes away, some other geezer would have had his arm. Before the week was out, the Giant would be part of someone's back-garden path.

When they were doing the Commonwealth Games in Manchester in 2002, they redeveloped the canal path from the city centre up to the new stadium and laid down this really nice York stone one day. They came back the next day and it was gone. Someone had it away overnight. As quick as they could lay it down, they kept on having it away. Some unsuspecting accountant or footballer in Cheshire has probably got a lovely York stone patio he paid good money for, and in reality it's just the nicked canal path from the Commonwealth Games.

Apparently you can see Bolivia from the top of the Atacama Giant. You can see for miles, that's for sure, but it is pretty much just desert so fuck knows if we're looking at Bolivia or not.

It's a mad thing to see, the Atacama Giant, but I'm not sure I'm as convinced as Nicolás that it's an alien astronaut that an ancient tribe had seen and then re-created in rocks. Maybe one of them saw a vision of something, but I'm not sure how much I can count this as hard, solid evidence of UFOs.

CHAPTER 8

I See Another UFO

THE DAY AFTER our trip to check out the Atacama Giant, I'm back in the desert again to investigate one of the most talked-about UFO cases in Chilean history. Back in 1977, the leader of a Chilean military patrol, Corporal Armando Valdés, was abducted one night in front of the rest of his patrol. Over thirty-five years after it happened, it is still one of the most famous UFO cases in Chile and it's talked about all over the world.

On the night of 25 April 1977, near a remote outpost called Pampa Lluscuma (close to the border with Peru), Valdés and his boys were on a night patrol and sitting around a campfire in the early hours when they saw an amazing bright light descend from the sky. They all shit themselves. As he was the geezer in charge, Valdés decided it was on his toes to investigate, so 'after praying to God and ordering the light to leave ... after demanding that it identify itself, I moved a few metres away from my men'.

But then he just disappeared in front of his pals. Gone. Disappeared. No sign of him. He eventually reappeared fifteen minutes later, but he was totally freaked out and start shouting at his pals, 'You don't know who we are or where we come from, but we will be back soon ...' Then he collapsed and passed out. He had been clean-shaven when he disappeared fifteen minutes earlier, but now he had a bloody beard. When he woke up later he said to his pals, 'I don't remember anything from the moment I left you.' He then ordered them, 'Get ready to leave because it's 4.30 a.m.' But it was actually 7 a.m. by that time. His watch had stopped at 4.30 a.m. but had somehow advanced five days and said 30 April instead of the 25th. All very strange.

Bear in mind this was Chile in 1977, so the dictator Augusto Pinochet was in charge, who was a no-messing kind of dude. Pinochet was Commander-in-Chief of the Army and had overthrown the government in a coup in 1973, and then he was made president by the junta. His government are believed to have killed a couple of thousand people and tortured up to 30,000, so Pinochet wasn't a geezer to be messing around with. When people are being tortured for stepping out of line, it's probably going to make a corporal in the Army think twice about coming out and making up some outlandish claims about being abducted, isn't it?

We've arranged to meet Patricio Abusleme Hoffman,

an author who has written a book called *La Noche de los Centinelas* about the Valdés case. 'This is the case that made Chilean ufology known worldwide,' says Patricio. 'However, no one bothered to conduct a serious, in-depth investigation of the case. I took up the challenge in 2002, and it took me eight years to compile the protagonists' accounts and reassemble this "impossible story".'

We meet at the hotel and then head out into the desert to hook up with one of the guys who was in Valdés's patrol and witnessed what happened that night. Old Valdés himself doesn't give interviews any more. He became a born-again Christian and an evangelical teacher and doesn't want to talk about what happened that night.

The dude we're meeting is Humberto Rojas. The incident happened near Arica, a port in northern Chile – we're meeting him near there so we can get more of a feel of what took place that night. As we start the climb into the desert hills, the road feels a bit like Snake Pass, the road over the Pennines between Sheffield and Manchester, but then it quickly becomes more desolate. By the time we meet Humberto it's already getting dark. Our director, Wayne – who's a top bloke who's won two BAFTAs, as he likes to casually slip into conversation now and again – wants me to meet with Humberto at night, around the campfire out in the desert, so I can imagine what it was like for him and his pals back in the day. He didn't get his BAFTAs for nothing, you know.

Humberto seems a pretty cool dude, with his little

pork-pie hat perched on his head. He can't speak English so Patricio has to translate for us. He tells us how he and the rest of the patrol were sat around the campfire that night, 'telling stories, singing and telling jokes to pass the time and try to ignore the cold'.

Humberto remembers his pal Pedro Rosales seeing the light first and screaming, and then giving them a shout to come and look. Humberto ran outside with his other pals to find a large, incredibly bright object moving around in the sky about 600 metres up the valley from where they were stood.

'The light came down and before it touched the hillside, another light came out of the big one. That light that passed before us illuminated the whole area, it was lit up as if it was daytime. We all held hands because we didn't know what it was ...'

Never mind Humberto and his pals holding hands back then, old Humberto is obviously still freaked out about it because, as he's telling me all this, he gets proper emotional and starts grabbing hold of my arm. I'm like, 'All right, easy, mate.'

I was a teenager when I had my first encounter back in the seventies and I wasn't really scared. But maybe I would have been scared if it had happened to me when I was older.

Humberto remembers, 'Valdés asked the light to identify itself. He commanded it in the name of God to identify itself ... and there was total silence. Suddenly we realized we had lost Valdés.'

When he was interviewed after the incident, Valdés said it was as if he had been 'swallowed by the light'.

As I said earlier, when Valdés reappeared fifteen minutes later, he was in a bit of a state.

'Suddenly Valdés fell in front of us,' Humberto tells me. 'Valdés was crying and calling for his mother. His eyes were wild. Then he started shouting: "You don't know who we are or where we come from, but we will be back soon . . ."'

Sitting round the campfire here, under the desert sky, it's impossible not to get swept up in Humberto's account of what happened that night. As with any old campfire story, there's some debate about the finer details, and I ask Humberto what he thinks was going on.

'I really believe they were UFOs. I think we are not alone in the galaxy. I think that the sensation never leaves you, you always feel like you are being watched from the skies.'

I do believe there is something to Humberto's story and he seems like a salt-of-the-earth bloke to me.

Shaun's X-Files

Bizarre phenomena of the 'Missing Time' kind experienced by Corporal Valdés are often associated with alien abduction, the most contentious side of ufology. Another of the most famous examples is the case of Betty and Barney Hill, who I mentioned earlier (although I'm a bit suspicious about their story). The first widely reported alien abduction in the USA, it's supposed to have taken place in 1961. After seeing a cigar-shaped UFO whilst out driving, they awoke in their car to find their clothes ripped, their watches stopped at the same time and with apparently no memory of the previous two hours.

What's really freaky is that as Humberto finishes telling us his story, we spot a mysterious light in the night sky in the distance. We stop filming and all of us – me, Humberto, Patricio, my manager Warren, Wayne the director and all the film crew – just stand there, amazed at this strange light in the sky. It seems to be changing colour, from red to green, and moving, then stopping and then setting off again. Wayne is convinced it's a star but you can see why some people might mistake it for a UFO. He may be right, but it's refreshing to be in a country where many people's first instinct is to believe rather than disbelieve, and a timely reminder for me to keep my eyes on the sky for the rest of my trip.

★

Next morning we are back in Santiago, the capital. We're off to investigate what sounds like a properly bonkers story. Even by UFO standards, this case is properly off the hook. It's an alien-contact story that has been around in Chile since the 1980s and it's pretty wild, claiming that aliens aren't just visiting Earth, but living here among us.

Well, not exactly among us, but living on a 'secret island' off Chile. It all sounds pretty far out to me – a secret island full of aliens? Surely there aren't any secret islands now that we have all this satellite technology and Google Maps and what have you. 'Secret island' all sounds a bit Robinson Crusoe. But that's what I'm here in Chile for – to investigate some of the most bizarre things that are alleged to have happened here.

We've arranged to meet a geezer called Sergio Alacaya, who has spent fifteen years investigating this weird 'Friendship' case.

Shaun's X-Files

The first reported contact from the mysterious group calling themselves 'The Friendship' was in 1984, when a radio operator called Octavio Ortiz claimed to have made contact with a mysterious group claiming to be 'not of this world'. Many witnesses reported seeing UFOs off the coast of Chile around the same time, although this has been explained by the authorities as a French stratospheric balloon. The captain of a ship called *Mytilus II* also claimed he had been hired by 'some gringos', who took him to an island and 'outfitted his ship with strange equipment'. They told him they were associated with UFOs that had been spotted. Ever since, stories have persisted about an ethereal group of beings who live in secret on one of the thousands of remote islands in southern Chile who possess magical healing powers. Rumour has it that either they have regular contact with aliens, have aliens living with them or are part human, part alien.

I meet Sergio in a park overlooking Santiago. I ask him to explain more about the case. 'I think they are a scientific and religious community who have contact with extraterrestrials. That's my conclusion. But some people think there is a connection between the Friendship and Nazis.'

Aliens and Nazis? This story just gets wilder.

Sergio explains that one of the alternative theories about the Friendship community is related to the influx of Germans and Italians who fled Europe after the Second World War. There're even a few people who believe that the Friendship are involved in trying to rebuild the Third Reich in southern Chile, although Sergio isn't convinced this is the case. I'm not having any of it either. I know there were a load of Nazis that poured into South America after the Second World War, and I referenced it in the first Black Grape single, 'Reverend Black Grape':

> Oh Pope, he got the Nazis
> To clean up their messes
> In exchange for gold and paintings
> He gave them new addresses
> Clean up your messes

But I'm not buying into this theory that those Nazis fleeing Europe ended up on a secret island off the coast of Chile and were in contact with aliens.

'My personal conclusion is there is no connection between the Friendship case and Nazis,' agrees Sergio.

'But you do believe there are humans on this island that are in contact with aliens?' I ask.

'Yes . . .'

He then loses me a bit with his next explanation, but from what I gather he is suggesting that female humans on the island bred with the aliens. Wow. The human beings bred with the aliens?

'Yes . . . they are a mix between human and extraterrestrial.'

Bloody hell. I don't quite know what to say to Sergio. The driving factor for Sergio's belief that the Friendship community have extraterrestrial links is his relationship with Ernesto de la Fuente, an ordinary geezer with an extraordinary claim.

We go to meet Ernesto to get his side of the story. Ernesto was one of the first people to contact the Friendship, via radio, and from the mid-1980s he developed a close link with the island community. Their relationship took an odd turn when, after falling ill in Santiago, Ernesto visited a doctor and was given some shocking news.

'I saw his face – he was worried – and he said, "Can you see here? Look here. You have cancer" . . . I couldn't believe it and I went home. And suddenly I found them in the radio. They told me, come here . . . maybe there is still time; and I went.'

Given just a matter of years to live, Ernesto decided to make the long 1,000-mile journey to southern Chile where he says he was met by the Friendship people. He fell asleep and was taken by boat to an island with just fourteen inhabitants and, he claims, buildings containing mysterious air-locked rooms. They gave him a secret treatment, which he says eradicated his cancer, although he never sought out official medical confirmation that he had been cured. 'I was coward enough not to ask. If I had cancer I would be dead by now.'

Almost thirty years later he's still alive and he believes that the treatment he received on that fateful trip in 1985 saved his life. He may not know where Friendship Island is but he carries a lasting memory of the people he met there.

'What I know is what they call the Friendship people, fourteen of them, don't get old. I believe the Friendship people are still on the island . . .'

Ernesto's story is pretty outlandish, but not knowing exactly where the island is hasn't stopped him and others thinking the Friendship community is still active. Sergio himself believes it's only a matter of time before we hear from them again.

To be honest, I'm struggling to accept all this. I really would love this to be true, to be real, and to believe that there's an island full of sophisticated, intelligent people who can cure cancer and are in relationships with aliens but I'm just not having it. Whatever the truth is about the Friendship case, I don't think it's got anything to do with UFOs.

★

I came to Chile looking for facts and confirmation behind the country's alien cases, but stuff like the Friendship case just feels more like a science-fiction story. We decide we need a bit more science-based investigation to get my UFO hunt back on track, so we decide to meet astronomer Lars-Åke Nyman to do just that. I feel like I'm going from one extreme to the other – from someone who believes a half-human half-alien race is living on a secret island to a top scientific bod who won't believe a thing unless he's got cold, hard evidence.

Shaun's X-Files
There are scientific reasons why extraterrestrials could be attracted to Chile. It's the best place in the world for communicating with distant galaxies, which is why it is home to most of the observatories in the southern hemisphere. ALMA (Atacama Large Millimeter/Submillimeter Array) is the largest astronomical project in the world, a joint project between the US, Japan and Europe, which was completed in 2013. ALMA is a revolutionary instrument in its scientific concept and engineering design, and as a global scientific project. The huge

listening device is located in the thin, dry air of northern Chile's Atacama Desert at an altitude of 5,000 metres above sea level. Made up of sixty-six high-precision antennae, it is opening a new window on the universe and allowing scientists to unravel important, longstanding astronomical mysteries.

Like I said earlier, Chile is one of the top places in the southern hemisphere for astronomers. Lars works on the ALMA project, the most recent in a long line of pioneering telescopes that have been built high in the Atacama Desert to take advantage of the clearest skies anywhere on Earth. As the largest astronomical project currently in existence, ALMA will allow unparalleled views of the cosmos. So there's one question I'm dying to ask Lars. Is there any chance his telescopes can detect life out there?

'Well, telescopes can maybe detect the building blocks of life, and then if they ever become sensitive enough to look at the atmosphere around planets in other solar systems, if we could detect water or oxygen or ozone, we would be able to tell if other life forms could exist on those planets, or at least it would give us an indication that there was a possibility for life.'

Shaun's X-Files

We can't see other planets outside our solar system yet, but there are other sophisticated ways of detecting them – and so far almost 3,000 have been found. This, however, is believed to be just a drop in the ocean. In 2012, NASA's Kepler satellite predicted our galaxy alone contains at least seventeen billion Earth-sized planets. If just a fraction of these support life, the implications are mind-blowing.

I, personally, think the universe is teeming with life. So, I put this to Lars. 'Given how many planets are out there, shouldn't life be pretty common?'

'That's right. But so far we haven't found life. We have sent some rovers and vehicles to Mars and tried. So far astronomers have detected more than 140 different types of molecules and some of them are quite complex, including sugars.'

Sugar? 'What has sugar got to do with it?' I ask Lars.

'Sugar is one of the building blocks of life. So it's interesting to find out that it is already out there in space, inside molecular clouds.'

'Do you believe that anyone is travelling between the stars?' I ask Lars. 'Do you think there are UFOs out there?'

'Personally, I don't think so. The distances between the stars are very, very large. Our nearest star is four light years away, so it takes light four years to travel here, so even if we could one day travel at the speed of light, it would take us a very long time to reach the nearest stars and stars beyond that.'

This is the thing that gets me, though – I reckon that scientists like Lars still think in terms of human technology. 'Can't we just open the fabric of time and space and, you know, just pop through it?'

'So far we have no indication that we can do those things,' he replies.

'But something like the craft that I saw when I was a teenager, that was defying the laws of gravity and zooming across the sky at 10,000 miles an hour, obviously had technology that was millions of years ahead of us. Surely they might be able to open up the fabric and step through?'

'This is speculation. But you don't know. I've spent twenty years standing on top of mountains looking at the sky and I've never seen anything I couldn't explain.'

'You should have come to Salford in the seventies, mate!' I tell him. Before I leave Lars, I ask him what his ultimate gut feeling is about life out there.

'I find it hard to believe that we would be the only unique life form in the universe . . . so many planets have been discovered, and molecules, that I think it is very likely that we will eventually find life on other planets.'

Lars has dedicated his life to studying the universe so it's great to hear him confirming that the probability of extraterrestrial life is so high. All right, so we might disagree on a few cosmic principles, but I feel my trip is back on track, and I think I'm miles better off concentrating on investigating what is happening in the skies above Chile, rather than searching for some secret island.

★

For my final trip in Chile, I decide I want to investigate another one of the country's top UFO hotspots in the hope that I can see something else mind-blowing before we head home. We have assembled a bit of a crack team to help us, including Antonio Huneeus and a research party from Chile's leading civilian UFO group, organized by Rodrigo Fuenzalida. We're driving in convoy south from Santiago to Colbún Lake, one of the well-known *zonas calientes* (UFO hotspots). Hopefully we're in good hands for my last throw of the intergalactic dice.

Rodrigo and his team are super keen, and they seem to have tipped off people about our mission. When we reach the *zonas calientes*, Rodrigo wants us to stop at a small UFO-themed roadside café (more of a shack really) and the guy who owns it, who seems to be some pal of Rodrigo, has laid on a spread to welcome me on this UFO mission. It's all a bit weird, it looks like the kind of spread you would put on for a kids' party, but in a small roadside UFO-themed shack, all to welcome me on my UFO hunt. I've got to say it's one of the weirdest receptions I've ever had. We can't stop long, though, as Wayne the director wants to get to Colbún Lake before sunset to make sure we're all set up for our big night of starwatching.

It's pretty stunning. Colbún's like a bigger, grander version of the Lake District, and there's a top sunset going down. The lake is actually the largest artificial reservoir in Chile, although you wouldn't necessarily know it was manmade just by looking at it. Rodrigo and Antonio tell me there has been a lot of UFO activity here and the locals partly put it down to the big power plant on the other side of the lake . . . they think the aliens are coming down and swiping power from the plant. They call them 'Light Stealers'. I'm not sure about this. If aliens have got the advanced technology and power to travel the galaxy and visit Earth, it seems pretty unlikely that once they're here they'll need to nick a bit of electricity to make sure they've got enough to get home. They probably don't even use electricity – wouldn't they have a more advanced energy?

Rodrigo tells me how his own team saw some UFOs in this exact spot, four years ago. They saw one hovering above the trees by the lodges where we are staying, and it was so low that it even burnt the top of the trees. Considering all the UFO sightings that have been reported here, it's difficult to believe we *won't* see something in the skies this evening.

Rodrigo's team moves in to set up the monitoring equipment and cameras in the hope that they will record any unusual activity in the night sky while we're kipping. His team all seem super keen, and I get the feeling that Rodrigo enjoys being in charge. They all take themselves pretty seriously. As the sun sets, I have a beer while they get organized, and it seems that all that's left for us to do is wait.

However, we then find out there is a major problem. Despite the fact that they take themselves so seriously, Chile's leading civilian UFO group have left a crucial bit of the kit back in Santiago. Which is really annoying. I was pretty excited about what we might capture on camera tonight. I thought we would get up in the morning and have nine hours of footage to go through. Instead, we're going to have nine hours of sweet Fanny Adams. I've come all this way and someone forgets a bit of kit. There's some debate about whether we can get someone to drive down from Santiago with the missing bit of kit, but it's a five-hour journey. The group phone round to see if anyone nearby will be able to help us, but we're in the middle of bloody nowhere and it's not the sort of thing a corner shop in the middle of bloody nowhere will stock, you know what I mean? With the equipment not working, the night feels like a dead loss – a pointless 250-mile trip to the middle of nowhere.

But just then, when we're all on a downer and on the verge of packing up and heading back to Santiago, I'm called over to look at a photo that Pancho, one of the film crew, has just taken of the night sky above us. Nothing could prepare me for what I'm about to see.

He's taken the picture on a long exposure and you can definitely see *something* come almost directly straight down, then shoot off at a right angle. Pancho has been taking pictures of the night sky in Chile for years, and as a rock climber he has been all over the world and he always takes pictures of the night sky when he is on his trips, but he says he has never seen anything like it. For me, it's definitely a UFO.

'Let's put it really simply,' I say.

'It's Unidentified . . .

'It's Flying . . .

'It's an Object . . .

'That makes it a fucking UFO, doesn't it?'

'I think it's a UFO too,' says Pancho, which surprises me a bit because I've had a slight vibe from Pancho all the while he's been with us that he has been taking everything with a pinch of salt.

Even my manager Warren, who is a total sceptic, is visibly shaken and believes it's a UFO. I'm made up that we've captured this on camera. This is more than I could have hoped for from this trip – proof of an actual UFO. We check the camera to rule out a damaged lens, and it's fine.

To me, what we captured on camera tonight is another sign that life exists out there in the universe. I know many people remain sceptical about UFOs, but we once thought the Earth was flat; perhaps it'll take a similar sea-change in our collective consciousness for humans to accept that we're not alone.

CHAPTER 9

The World's Most Famous
Alien Abductee

BACK FROM CHILE, I now wanted to take a look at our opinion and reaction to UFO stories at home. I decided I wanted to take a closer look at some of the UK's most famous and infamous UFO cases from over the years. I was interested to find out a bit more about them, and meet the people involved, and see how it had affected them.

The press can be quite sensationalist when it comes to reporting UFOs. Unlike in South America or other parts of the world that are more open-minded, in the UK sightings are often treated with scepticism. Depending on what sort of person you are, any encounter can knock you for six, and if you find yourself in the media spotlight it must make it even harder to deal with. It can't help, when you're trying to make sense of what's happened to you, to have all sorts of people questioning your account. I wanted to learn a bit more about some of the UK's best-known UFO stories, and also to see how the witnesses have coped.

To help me out on this UFO road trip across Britain, I've enlisted America's most famous abductee, Travis Walton. As I mentioned earlier, I've followed Travis's incredible story for years so when we started work on the TV show, Travis was one of the first names on my team sheet of people that I wanted involved in the programme. When our researchers got in touch with him, he said he was happy to come over to the UK and get involved in the show. So I'm really looking forward to going on a UFO road trip with him.

Travis's extraordinary account provoked a media storm back in 1975. On 5 November, as I said, he was working with a logging crew in a remote corner of Arizona, but this is what happened that night. On the way home they saw a bright light behind a hill and when they drove closer they saw a large, silvery disc hovering above a clearing and shining brightly. It was around eight feet high and twenty feet across. They stopped the truck and Travis decided to get out and take a closer look. As he approached the spacecraft, the others saw a beam of blue-green light coming from the disc and 'strike' him. They shit themselves and sped off into the night. But after driving for a while, they realized they couldn't leave Travis and went back for him. There was no sign of Travis or the flying saucer.

The logging crew drove back into town and reported the incident to the Deputy Sheriff, who said they were all distraught when they told him what had happened. The whole town searched for Travis for days and, when news got out about what had happened, news teams and UFO researchers all turned up. Then five days later, Travis reappeared a few miles from where he was allegedly taken, and described coming face-to-face with alien beings aboard some kind of craft.

The fact that both he and other members of the crew have passed numerous polygraph tests over the years makes this, without doubt, the most believable incident I've ever come across.

Travis has spent his life sharing his ordeal with others who claim to have had similar experiences. He only very rarely comes to the UK, and I feel his wealth of knowledge on this trip is going to prove invaluable.

Travis meets me in a recording studio in Manchester called Blueprint Studios, where I am just finishing work on a recording. It's actually in Salford, and everyone from Timbaland to REM has recorded there.

As soon as I meet Travis, I like him, straightaway. I think he's a totally straight-up dude, just a normal regular guy. He's not an egomaniac. He doesn't have this desperation for publicity that a lot of people that I come across do. I'm starting to see that there are some people in the UFO game that have egos as big as people in the music game. It's weird the effect that the slightest bit of attention has on some people – it's like a drug, they just want more and more. I've never been like that, I've never craved the attention. I know it sounds weird for the frontman of a band to say, but I've never been completely comfortable being at the centre of things. As I've said, that was one of the main reasons I first got Bez up on stage with Happy Mondays, all those years ago, to deflect the focus from me.

Travis seems a bit similar in a way. It's like he's accepted that there is always going to be interest in his case and what had happened to him, but he doesn't exactly crave the attention or get a buzz off it. He's a breath of fresh air, really. He comes across as totally genuine. You can tell he's gone through some really traumatic experience. In some of his interviews back in the seventies, shortly after the incident happened, he looks shell-shocked. He looks like he's got post-traumatic stress disorder, like a young soldier who has just come back from Vietnam or Northern Ireland. One look at him in those early interviews and you can tell he's been through a terrifying experience. It's not only the look in his eyes, which is a bit of a thousand-yard stare. But also the way he speaks, the way he acts, everything. He looks traumatized.

Because I know all this about him before we meet, and because he must be sick of people bombarding him with the same old questions as soon as they meet him, I deliberately don't jump in straightaway with questions. I decide to just hang out with him for the first day or so, and we have a bit of a laugh and a joke. I just play it the way I'd like someone to play it with me. It does my head in when someone I first meet starts saying, 'What was it like when you did this with the Mondays?', 'Tell me what Bez is really like?', 'Did you really take all those drugs?', 'What was it like in the jungle?' Blah, blah, blah. That's the worst way to start off with anyone, bombarding them with questions, because they'll just think you're a bit of an idiot. I always prefer to hang out with someone first.

Fair play to Travis, he's a trooper. The guy is in his fifties and he'd flown into London late the night before, gone to some average hotel the production company had stuck him in, and only had a McDonald's for tea that night. Then he'd got on an early train from London to meet us up north. Fair play to the geezer, that's a pretty hardcore schedule for someone who's no spring chicken, and he didn't complain at all. So straightaway you know he's a decent geezer.

The first place me and Travis are off to investigate on our UFO road trip round the country is High Bentham in North Yorkshire, up near the Lake District. If you'd have asked me without showing me a map, I would have said this was Lancashire, being north up the M6 from Manchester, but apparently it's North Yorkshire. I never realized it spread so far west. It's a nice part of the world, all rolling green hills and small villages here and there, just like the scenery in that Steve Coogan and Rob Brydon programme *The Trip*. It's hardly Roswell, but this unassuming place was the setting of an intriguing UFO case in 2007.

Most UFO sightings are reported by individuals, but what makes this case unusual is that a whole family claim to have had a shared UFO encounter. There were also other witnesses from the surrounding area that said they saw something that night and corroborated the Deverow family's sighting, which led to a brief flurry of media interest.

The four family members were Anne, her daughter Rachel and Rachel's two sons, Alex and Benjamin, who were aged nine and eleven when it happened. They'd been for a meal out at a Little Chef and were on their way home when it happened.

They suddenly became aware of a bright white light in the sky to their left. They described the object as being about the size of a car headlight and being so bright that it made the moon look yellow. The object then moved across the sky and became visible through the windscreen, then went upwards and hovered right above their car. At this point the light accelerated downwards at an amazing speed. It was so fast that the family braced themselves for impact but it never occurred. Instead, the object gained altitude again and sped away over the hills of the Forest of Bowland. While this was happening, they all just watched without saying anything – they didn't say a word until the strange object had disappeared from view. The next thing they remembered was driving into the village of High Bentham, where they lived. Anne rang up Radio Lancashire the next morning and they got her on air to describe what had happened to her, and lots of other witnesses came forward and said they had seen something similar, although they hadn't had the same close experience that the Deverow family had.

Seven years on, they all still live in the same High Bentham farmhouse and have agreed to meet me and Travis to talk us through the weird experience that happened to them that night. They recount the story to us, and Nana explains how 'beautiful' the peculiar object looked, and how she felt an 'overpowering love' for it. Rachel adds that after it disappeared they were all desperate to see it again.

They also explain that they went back to where it happened six days later to try and retrace their steps. The weird thing was that the journey only took them nine minutes, whereas it had taken over half an hour on the night of the incident, which made their experience a 'missing time' episode.

Shaun's X-Files

The manifestations may differ between cultures, but one factor reported in many UFO experiences is the phenomenon of 'missing time', a gap in the conscious memory of the people at the centre of these events. Another well-respected case, not that dissimilar to the Deverow family's incident, also involved a group driving home from dinner together, and took place in Kentucky on 6 January 1976. As Mona Stafford and her two friends were driving, a bright-red object appeared in the sky, which Mona at first thought was an airplane on fire. As the object descended from the right side of the road to a point ahead of them, they could see that it wasn't an airplane, but a huge object bigger than 'two houses'. All the women described it as an enormous, metallic, disc-shaped object with a dome on top and a ring of red lights around the middle. The women all saw the disc close enough to see a yellow, blinking light on its underbelly. They realized they were driving at 85 mph, faster than they had ever driven before, and they were convinced the spaceship had taken control of their car. They later came back to consciousness on the highway, driving in the same direction, but realized with horror that they couldn't account for well over an hour of time, raising the possibility that they were temporarily abducted.

The Deverow family's account is beginning to sound plausible to me, but I know from my own experience of telling people about my UFO incidents that most people won't have taken their story seriously.

Alex, the youngest lad, says, 'At school I tried telling everyone what happened but as you can imagine I just got laughed at. It's so crazy that people don't want to believe that it happened.'

His older brother agrees. 'I think that people are very close-minded, and very quick to reject the idea that an incident might have happened. Even though it's difficult for me to comprehend and it doesn't really make sense and is unlike anything that has happened to me before, I still acknowledge that it happened, I know it happened. I don't think you can truly believe anyone about an incident like this until you've witnessed one yourself.'

Anne asks Travis if it helped him to talk to people who had had similar experiences.

'I think it does. But back when it happened to me, there was hardly anything in the way of support groups. I went to a few conferences and was pretty freaked out by the strangeness I saw there, so I kind of avoided that. But it's improved and more people who have witnessed things are coming forward. It's less traumatic now than it was.'

As me and Travis talk to the family, I realize that the older kid is taking the experience from more of a scientific point of view, trying to be pragmatic about it. Maybe he's a little bit embarrassed about admitting in public what he thinks he saw, and he's trying to rationalize it a bit. When something dramatic and otherworldly happens to you, obviously you try and find an explanation for it. You're racking your brains, searching for an answer. You're trying to impose a rational framework on to something that is pretty bloody irrational, which doesn't work.

I've tried to do that with the incidents that have happened to me, and Travis says that he's tried to do that as well. He has quite a good take on things, Travis, and it's good to have him with me to bounce ideas off. He tells me and the family how he eventually decided not to stick a label on what happened to him. He decided he was just going to stick to describing exactly what happened and let other people label it how they saw fit.

The brothers seem to agree that once you've seen something, and have accepted that you've seen something, then you are probably more susceptible to seeing something else. Their nana backs them up and says, 'It opens your mind and it can only be a good thing.'

Travis agrees: 'You're more accepting of ambiguity, and I think that's a good thing.'

I like the family and I believe them, but I get the feeling they are maybe holding something back, as if they don't want to say exactly how they feel about what happened on camera. Which you can understand if they are still coming to terms with it a little bit.

They seem a nice, normal family and what I think makes their story more believable is the fact that they all have a very slightly different take on it. If you had four people at a football match and asked them to describe what happened, then you would get a difference of opinion, wouldn't you? If you asked the Mondays to describe a gig that we had just played then I can fucking guarantee you that you would get a difference in opinion. You'd probably think we were all talking about different gigs.

You also find that people react differently in different situations, particularly when something shocking or something you can't explain happens. I know what human nature is like. When it comes to it there are different types of people who react differently in situations when you put them under pressure. Say a massive bang goes off unexpectedly, then some people will crouch and hide, and some people will jump up and immediately try and work out what has happened and confront the situation if necessary.

During the interview, I can tell Travis feels an empathy with the family because he opens up to them more than to most other people. He especially seems to relate to the fact that some people have taken the piss out of the story of their experience. 'Condemnation without investigation is the highest form of ignorance,' he reassures the family. The thing is, you'll find that half those people who take the piss out of you will later come back, maybe when there're fewer people around, and ask you more about what happened, and they're actually really interested. Rachel, the mum, says she's had similar reactions as well.

We also talk a little bit about how some of the loons and goons that UFO conferences and events attract don't exact help the public perception of people who have seen something. Travis says he's been to plenty of conferences where there are talks given by really serious people who have pretty strong evidence to support their stories or their sightings, but then there will generally always be some goon in a ten-gallon hat. Half the time he'll be the one who ends up being on TV just because they think it's a better or funnier story, as opposed to something which might open people's minds and get them to think a bit. 'What are these conference organizers supposed to do?'

Travis asks me. 'Have some sort of litmus test for lunatics? There are several well-known cases that in my opinion are absurd.' That must get mega frustrating for old Travis, having to regularly go up against all these nutcases that he knows are making stuff up. Travis is such a nice, friendly dude, it's difficult to imagine him getting hassled about anyone, but that must cabbage his head a bit. As if he's not annoyed enough with people questioning his story and him having to defend it, he also sometimes has to defend it against a background of fruitcakes. He must think, 'Don't label me with these dudes, man.'

I must say the Deverow family all seem very sane and level-headed to me, and I make sure I tell them that. Travis and I are eager to make sense of what happened that evening, so we ask them to take us out to the area where the incident happened.

In the days following the incident, Rachel and Anne returned to the site in an attempt to piece together what had happened to them and the boys. But despite being convinced they knew where they saw the light, try as they might they were unable to find any stretch of the road that matched their memory of events. Which freaked them out quite a bit, obviously.

Shaun's X-Files

Some level of amnesia or reality distortion is not uncommon in those who claim to have seen UFOs, but rather than the symptom of a traumatic experience, some ufologists have a theory that these cases shared by individuals may be explained by some kind of extraterrestrial mind control. I'm not sure about that.

There was a lot that the family aren't prepared to say on camera, but which they talk to me about afterwards. Anne and Rachel actually went for regression therapy after the event, because they couldn't work out what had gone on. When they went for regression therapy they realized that the road they were driving along when the incident happened was not a real road on Earth, but a road in the sky, and they were in a UFO. Which would explain why they couldn't find the road when they went back looking for it, and would also explain the missing time that they couldn't account for. But they didn't want to talk about that on camera.

★

After we leave the family, Travis and I chat a bit more about how people prejudge you and how some people are never going to believe anything out there exists. You have to judge each case on its own merit. Travis agrees, or as he puts it: 'It's nonsense to say that it's all real or it's all baloney.' He also says that a lot of people have come up to him over the years and told him that the fact that he has talked so publicly about his experience has helped them, because they had also seen something. 'In that sense, I'm not alone,' he says.

'This is so hard to do,' he explains, meaning talking in public about his experience. 'But it's got less traumatic than it was. It's got to the stage where I guess I'm a little desensitized.'

I'm starving, so I decide to nip into the nearest village, which is Kirkby Lonsdale, and let Travis experience that old English delicacy, fish'n'chips. I tell him about how me mam and dad had a chippy for a year, when I was a kid in the seventies. They were ahead of the game because they were the first chippy round our way to serve curry sauce. This chippy in Kirkby Lonsdale has steak and kidney pudding and I'm tempted to have one, but they aren't Holland's. The film crew, who are all from down south, have never even heard of steak pudding! The whole concept of a pudding with meat is weird to them. I explain to them what a pudding is, and how if you're going to have a pudding, it's got to be Holland's.

Travis enjoys his fish'n'chips and even has a cup of tea to wash it down. It's the third cup of tea he's had today – he must be the most English Yank I've ever met, even though he's only been here once.

The teasing the boys had got at school was typical, but it's got a lot better over the years. Even the media, especially the tabloids, have stopped relentlessly taking the piss out of anyone who claims to have had some sort of UFO experience.

What was a little weird was that all the family talked about the overwhelming love towards the thing that they saw, and Rachel and Anne both said they really wanted to see another one. I can totally identify with that. I wouldn't say that when I had my experiences I felt an overwhelming love towards the craft, but I certainly didn't feel threatened by it.

The other thing is that time does change your feelings about an experience. You will probably feel different about something three, five or ten years later. Especially the boys, who were only nine and eleven years old when it happened. Even though they know what they saw, they're not standing up and saying they believe in UFOs – they're looking for a more scientific explanation for it all. Over our chippy tea, Travis points out to me that the older kid, Benjamin, said something about embellishment, and he wondered if he might even be talking about his mum and nana: Benjamin wants to stick to the facts. But as the boys grow older, I think they may find that no matter how hard they try, they won't be able to explain what happened to them through looking at conventional science, and they'll end up accepting that they had some sort of UFO experience.

I really did believe their story. One thing that helped convince me was that Rachel, the mother, has a pretty high-flying job. She's a representative for a pharmaceutical company, and she's obviously really intelligent and together, but she's had this experience with the rest of her family that she can't quite understand.

Travis is with me on this – he believed the family too. He was convinced they'd definitely had some sort of experience; he was having it.

The thing is, they had a collective experience, which changes other people's perceptions. The former clinical psychologist and UFO expert Peter McCue has talked quite a bit about how people are more likely to believe in collective experiences than individual experiences. One of the things that he's said is that even if you give four people acid and they all have hallucinations at the same time, none of them would have the same hallucination, so a group of people all witnessing the same thing happening at the same time can't be put down to a hallucination.

Which makes sense, although I do take what McCue says with a pinch of salt. He's obviously a bright geezer and he has a lot of decent theories – he's made me think about some things in a different way and I intend to talk to him in person as part of my research. But I'm also wary that he's seized the opportunity to become a bit of an expert in his field by applying his psychological experience to the paranormal.

When we set off on this trip I thought I knew all there was to know about Travis's story, but now I've met him and hung out with him, it's made me think a bit more about how much his UFO experience might have fundamentally affected him. Over our tea, he reveals to me that if he could rewind history and do things differently, or if he had to do it all again, he's not sure if he would tell anyone had happened to him.

He's obviously been through a lot over the years, and it must do your head in when something so life-changing happens to you and a lot of people's reaction is to question whether it actually happened at all.

I can see why he decided to take a step back from it all. Right after it happened he was like the John Lennon of the UFO world in America. He was just bombarded by the press and TV – everyone wanted to speak to him and interview him. Can you imagine? Before it all happened, he was happy as Larry being a lumberjack from some small town. Just getting on with his own life. Then out of nowhere he's abducted for five days. As if his head is not in a spin already from his encounter, he's then thrown into this whirlwind of TV shows and newspaper interviews. It's enough to cabbage anyone's head, and it obviously cabbaged Travis's for a while. But he felt he had to go out and do all those interviews because the incident had been so widely reported and everyone had an opinion on it, all the so-called experts – and you know my opinion on some of these so-called experts – and a lot of them obviously were picking holes in it. Travis naturally felt he had to put his version of events forward. He was constantly grilled for ten years, with half of the people thinking he was some kind of hero and the other half basically calling him a liar or a loon. That's how it goes with these type of stories from my experience – you've got the absolute nuts who will lap up anything you tell them, and then you've got the absolute sceptics, who'll have none of it and just think what you're saying is bollocks. There's no middle ground, and Travis was trapped in that crossfire.

Fuck me. It would do anyone's head in, so no wonder he stepped out of the limelight.

Now we have spent a bit of time together, and have got pretty comfortable with each other, we start chatting more openly about stuff and I'm finding out more about his story. You find out more from someone if you get to know them a bit by just casually chatting than if you just barge in there straight off with a load of questions.

Part of the reason why the caricature of the Mondays, and me and Bez in particular, lasted so long was that no one who was ever sent to interview us actually bothered to try and see further than that caricature. Which suited us at the time. We knew that those rock'n'roll tales of excess made for good headlines, and it's a piece of piss to throw a journalist a few tales about excess, isn't it? And it made our life easier as we didn't have to do any soul-searching or anything. But I always thought it was fucking poor on the journalists' part, that they just turned up wanting a few clichéd rock'n'roll tales and then they would run away happy to write the same piece that had been written a million times before about the mad world of Happy Mondays. Maybe it's because most of them were nice middle-class kids, from a nice upbringing, who had genuinely never met anyone like us – some of them had never even met a northerner – but, fuck me, it wasn't half boring.

Anyway, having got to know Travis better, that's when he tells me more about what actually happened when he was abducted. He says there were two types of aliens on the ship. There were these little thumb-faced dudes, and then there were these six-foot, blonde-haired, blue-eyed, more humanoid-looking creatures, who didn't seem to speak. I wonder if the tall humanoid creatures might have even been holograms, if they weren't speaking. If the little thumb-faced creatures are a race that are a million years more advanced than us, then they could even have created the holograms to have something more humanoid knocking about to make Travis feel more comfortable. They could have been something they knocked up in a lab that day. In the film of Travis's encounter, *Fire in the Sky*, there was only one type of creature, who looked like a big toe with eyeballs – a kind of bastardized mix of the two types he saw.

In the car on the way back to Manchester, Travis tells me about some of the weirdest things that have happened to him through his fame. He tells me about a Swedish death-metal band called Hypocrisy that have written a song about Travis called 'Fire in the Sky'. I pull it up on YouTube and watch it with Travis, and we have a bit of a laugh because it's pretty bloody awful. It has those deep rasping vocals that I wouldn't call singing, because you haven't a clue what they're saying. You can't pick out a word – you wouldn't even know it's called 'Fire in the Sky' – but we Googled the lyrics and it was all about Travis's experience.

Travis also tells me about a few other songs that have been written about him, including 'Why'd They Had to Let Me Out in Tucson' by Lewis Wickham, an old country and western tune that was written just after the incident in 1975. It didn't happen in Tuscon, but old Lewis Wickham was told it did. Travis also said there's a song by Pete Kozak, also called 'Fire in the Sky'. I had no idea there were songs about Travis, but it's not that surprising given than he is the most famous abductee ever.

CHAPTER 10

Call the Cops

HOPEFULLY YOU'VE GOT the idea by this point that although there are a certain amount of loons in the UFO business, I'm not out to take the piss out of anyone. There are so many wild and wacky stories out there, but I wanted to make sure the ones we concentrated on were fascinating – the ones that couldn't be explained away because they were told by some prime nutters living in cloud cuckoo land.

After our adventures in North Yorkshire with the Deverow family, the next day we're off to West Yorkshire to investigate an incident that happened back in 1980 in Todmorden. This part of the Pennines has had quite a few sightings over the years – the Calder Valley has become known as 'UFO Alley' to some people due to a wave of sightings that date back as far as the 1970s. I find it a pretty odd part of the world anyway. It's quite desolate but pretty beautiful in a raw way.

First, we have to film some links for a Facebook page – just one of those things you have to do in this day and age. As I've said, I don't have a Facebook page myself – can you imagine the nutters it would attract if I did? – but the TV series has a Facebook page so they want me to record a few pieces to camera, just saying, 'Hi, I'm Shaun Ryder, blah blah', which is easy enough. Apart from the fact that it's pissing down. Our director is from Texas and our sound guy is Canadian, and even though they both live over here, they live down south and can't quite believe how grim the weather is. I'm like, mate, the weather is like this for ten months of the year in this part of the world, from Rochdale down the valley to Todmorden – it always seems to be at least drizzling. Peter Kay calls it 'that fine rain that soaks you through' and it is, it's deceptive, and it means you're always a bit cold and damp. The sound guy complains that 'this rain and wind just permeates you'. I promise you it's colder in Todmorden than it was up the Andes, certainly today.

I nail these pieces to camera pretty quickly and then we drive back into the centre of Todmorden. We're here to investigate one of the UK's most renowned UFO incidents, but first we want to gen up on all the reports of the incident from the time, so me and Travis nip into Tod library to discover whether the local papers hold any clues. Weird gaffs, libraries, especially nowadays. Who goes to a library now, when everything is available online? Having said that, the old dears who run Todmorden Library and knew we were coming are super helpful. They've even arranged some tea and coffee for us in their staff room, where there is a computer that is so old school it has got a floppy-disc drive. Looks like it should be in a museum rather than a library. We're not using that to search on today, though – we're going even more old school and using microfiche.

When the incident happened it was first reported in the *Todmorden News & Advertiser*, so Travis and me look up the articles on microfiche. I've never used microfiche before but you see reporters and police using it to look at old newspapers in films. I didn't really think people still looked things up on microfiche in the real world; you presume everything is archived online nowadays, don't you? Can't we just bloody Google it? Then again, no disrespect, but I suppose the *Todmorden News & Advertiser* is not exactly the *New York Times*, so maybe there's not the demand.

While we're waiting for the librarians to set it up for us, I tell Travis that when I saw one of the earliest filmed interviews with him, I thought he looked like a man with post-traumatic stress disorder. Travis says that's not surprising because he was shell-shocked by what had happened. He's a pretty chilled guy now though, Travis. Almost a little bit Zen, I think you could say. He still seems pretty affected by it, but I suppose you would if you'd been abducted by aliens.

I ask Travis if he'd heard of the Todmorden case back home in the States and he said no, probably because he had enough to cope with just dealing with his own case and what happened to him. He kept himself to himself for years and in the end tried to ignore what was going on in the ufology world. But he had read up on the case once he knew we were going to be investigating it.

Anyway, the old dears at the library show us how to use the microfiche. It's pretty weird at first, but I soon get the hang of it and I find what we're looking for. There are actually two cases that happened in Todmorden in 1980, but there's one man who connects them both.

The headline for the first news story in the *Todmorden News & Advertiser* is 'Riddle of body found in Goods Yard'.

On the afternoon of Wednesday, 11 June 1980, a man's body was found lying on top of a big coal tip in a goods yard in Todmorden. There were no footmarks to indicate that anyone had climbed the twelve-foot high heap of coal to put the body there, or that the bloke had climbed up there himself and then died. It was as if it had been dropped from the sky somehow.

Two Todmorden coppers, PC Alan Godfrey and a colleague, arrived at the scene at 4.10 p.m. The body was clean, as if the man had just had a shower, but there were weird marks on the back of his head, neck and shoulders where the skin had been burnt off. The precise cause of the burns was unknown but it was possibly some sort of corrosive agent.

On seeing the burns, and finding his wallet, watch and shirt missing (the rest of his clothing was intact), Alan and his pal immediately suspected a crime, and the police investigation began. In the first news report, the day after this poor geezer was found, there wasn't any mention of a possible link to UFOs. It was just a pretty straightforward news report. The UFO link came later.

No one had even worked out who the poor dude was yet as the report said, 'Police were yesterday trying to discover the identity of the man who was described as having a shaven head probably because of a skin complaint from which he suffered.' The official line from the Old Bill to the press was, 'We are not applying any suspicious circumstances to this body yet', but they always bloody say that, don't they? If a dead body with weird marks on it found semi-clothed on top of a massive coal heap isn't suspicious then I don't know what is.

The poor dude was later identified as a fifty-seven-year-old Polish coal miner called Zygmunt Adamski. Top name or what? Some handle that. I don't think he was related to Adamski who had the Number One with Seal in 1990, who I played with one or twice with Happy Mondays. This Adamski – or Zyggy as I started calling him because it was easier – was from Tingley, near Wakefield, which is about thirty miles away. Apparently, old Zyggy was a normal loving family man, and he'd popped out to buy some potatoes (that's what the press said, I'm not taking the piss) for dinner on the previous Friday afternoon and never came back. The coroner said the actual cause of death was a heart attack. He reckoned that the weird burns marks on the back of his head, shoulders and neck, where the skin had been peeled away, were caused two days before he died. There were also traces of a greasy substance on the burns, possibly an ointment that had been used to treat the wounds. Apparently they sent it away to be analysed at some lab or wherever they send things, but whoever the geezer was who analysed it had no fucking idea – he'd never seen anything like it.

The specialists reckoned he'd been dead for about twenty-four hours before he was found, and he only had one day's growth of beard. The whole thing was weird. His wounds were two days old but he only had one day's growth of beard? What, so he'd had a shave after his head and shoulders were burnt? Zyggy's family also said he had thick black hair when he went missing, but his head was shaved when he was found.

To top that, his clothes were fairly clean. Which they wouldn't be if he'd clambered up a massive coal heap. And the lack of any footmarks up the coal heap was very strange. Have you ever tried to climb up a coal heap? It's impossible. Imagine trying to climb up a massive coal heap carrying a dead body. It just isn't happening mate, so there's no way someone else carried and dumped poor old Zyggy up there. Weird.

The medical examination concluded that death occurred somewhere between 11.15 a.m. and 1.15 p.m. that day, and the body had been on the coal tip beside a busy railway line for perhaps three or four hours before it was discovered. His widow believed that he had been kidnapped and tortured. The inquest returned a verdict of 'death caused by heart failure due to a shock or fright'.

To this day the death of old Zyggy remains unsolved. He had been missing for five days when his body was discovered on top of the coal heap; the same amount of time Travis disappeared for. When they did the post-mortem, the coroner, James Turnbull, said it was 'the most bizarre case he'd ever come across', and I imagine coroners have seen some bizarre things in their time.

Turnbull said, 'The question of where he was before he died and what led to his death just could not be answered.'

As I said earlier, there is a long history of weird activity along the Calder Valley, and there had even been some weird orange-glowing balls spotted near Todmorden around this time. The incident was linked by some to UFOs.

This is where the story gets slightly weirder. A few months after Zyggy was found, PC Alan Godfrey, one of the coppers who had attended the scene, had an experience of his own.

★

Alan was on the nightshift on 28 November 1980 when he saw a UFO on Burnley Road, near Todmorden Cricket Club. He was on his own, but other coppers also reported seeing something similar. Three coppers from

Halifax were up on the moors and spotted this bright blue light, which moved very quickly from north to south, then from east to west.

Just before dawn Alan was driving along Burnley Road near the park on the edge of Todmorden, looking for some cows that had been reported missing. Around 5 a.m., he was about to give up searching for the cows and head back to base to finish his shift when he saw 'a large mass' a few hundred yards ahead. At first, he thought it was an early morning bus coming towards him, as he knew there was one due about that time that took workers to their jobs in town. But when he got within twenty-five yards of the object, he realized it was not a vehicle on the road, but a craft hovering five feet off the ground. He tried calling for backup but his car radio wasn't working, and his personal radio was also 'completely dead'. Alan could also see that the craft was emitting some kind of force that was disrupting the trees on either side of the road, a bit like a helicopter, but it made no noise whatsoever and he couldn't feel any vibration in the police car.

For safety reasons, Alan stayed in the car and started to sketch the craft on his notepad. He described it as a diamond shape, with the bottom half rotating and the top stationary. But as he finished his sketch, he realized there had been a 'jump in time'; he suddenly found himself driving the car again, approximately twenty or thirty yards past the point at which he met the object. Alan came to the conclusion he had been abducted. He retraced his steps to check out where he had seen the craft and the road was dry, despite the fact that the rest of the road was wet with rain.

He went back to the police station and reported the incident, although some of his colleagues were sceptical.

The cows Alan had been looking for, by the way, were only found after sun-up, mysteriously relocated in a rain-soaked field without hoofmarks to indicate their passage. Alan reckoned the only way they could have got there would have been if they had been 'dropped from the sky'.

It was all very odd. The report in the paper had the headline, 'Amazing encounter in Calder Valley – May the Force be with you'.

Some of the press made the connection between Alan's sighting and old Zyggy's disappearance, and claimed there must be some extraterrestrial link between the two. Later, some fellow police officers suggested to Alan that he should undergo regression therapy to try and work out what had happened during his missing time. Despite initial reservations, he eventually agreed to do it. There's a video of the regression, which I've seen, and it's quite odd. Fair play to Alan, I'm not sure I'd want people to watch the video if that was me in it. He looks quite disturbed in the film – he's clearly really uncomfortable with what's going on, although it's hard to tell how much of that is down to what he's apparently remembering, and how much of it is down to him not being happy with the whole regression thing. It's in black and white as well, so it looks like a mixture between a very early episode of *Doctor Who* and a pilot episode of *Juliet Bravo*.

During the session, Alan claims that the UFO stopped his car engine, filled his radio with static and then blinded him with an intensely bright light, which caused him to lose consciousness. His next supposed memory was being inside a room that looked like it was in a normal house (although it was supposed to be on the craft). There was a large black dog and a geezer with a beard in the room, plus several small, robot-like creatures with heads shaped like light bulbs. The bearded geezer was dressed in 'biblical' clothes and communicated with Alan telepathically, revealing that his name was 'Yosef' and that Alan already 'knew' him. All very strange, isn't it? This geezer Yosef also promised Alan he was going to have another encounter.

Another local press cutting that we find talks about the huge interest in Alan's story around the world: 'Unassuming local bobby Alan Godfrey is "waiting for the dust to settle" before another attempt is made to plunder his memory in search of the answer to a UFO mystery.' It reveals that the thirty-four-year-old policeman had been 'hounded by Europe's media all week after hypnosis sessions revealed he might have met "space invaders" during a close encounter of the third kind'.

The UFO incident proved to be a huge turning point in Alan's life. He left the police force and now is a speaker at charity fundraising events. But it's not all been positive. In the past Alan has said, 'I wish I'd never seen the UFO, particularly because of the effects on my children . . . It's not easy having a policeman as a father but when he's a policeman who saw a UFO it's even worse.'

I can see that. Todmorden is a small town, so you can imagine when Alan was going about his business people were nodding and saying, 'There's that copper who reckons he was abducted' and stuff like that. I can see how it would be a nightmare for his kids as well. It would obviously be a talking point at the local school – 'Did your dad get abducted again last night?' Kids can be a nightmare, can't they?

The thing that freaks me is a picture of this dude Alan Godfrey alongside the report in the paper: he looks the absolute spit of Travis. Or what Travis must have looked like back then. It's very weird. Even though I've just met Travis I rib him a bit about it, but he's cool with it.

We find out that Alan is still living just outside Todmorden, between Walsden and a place called The Summit, so we decide to go and speak to him and get his version of events. Travis had never met Alan, but coincidentally they had both been filmed for the same TV show once.

Alan lives in a bungalow he built right on the Rochdale Canal. You can just sit at the kitchen table chilling out and watching the barges go past. Which I am quite into. This might surprise you, but I nearly bought a barge recently. Me and Joanne even took one for a test drive or whatever the equivalent of a test drive is for a barge. We went from Salford into Castlefield in central Manchester, which took about five hours, jumped off for a bit of lunch and then back on again. In fact, in Castlefield there's a nice gaff called Dukes 92, named after lock number 92, which is nearby. When me and Jo had the idea of getting a barge, we dreamt of just picking up the kids from school on a Friday, throwing 'em in the barge and just doing one for a nice chilled weekend. We quite fancied that. Having it barge. That's how chilled out I am when I'm at home now . . . I'd be quite happy to spend the weekend barging it than larging it. So even though we didn't end up buying the one that we took out for a test drive, we still haven't ruled out getting one.

Travis and me sit in Alan's kitchen and he tells us about the two incidents he was involved in and some stuff that never made the official reports or papers. He tells us about old Zyggy and what he looked like when he found him. 'He'd been missing for six days. We later found out he had thick, wavy hair when he'd gone missing but when he was found his hair looked like it had been cropped really roughly . . . and he had individual burn marks around his head, as if something was placed there [like a helmet or some sort of contraption, I think he meant]. Then as you turned his head over, there was also a hole in the back of Zyggy's neck, in the nape of the neck, which was smeared with some sort of ointment, like Vaseline or something.'

As we already knew, the ointment was sent away to the Home Office laboratories for assessment, but despite doing loads of tests, they had no idea what it was.

'When we went to the post-mortem the pathologist

was straightaway really taken aback by the look on his face. He suggested he had died of a heart attack, and he said to us, "You've heard the saying 'Frightened to death'? Well this is a typical example of it.'"

Alan stresses, 'That guy didn't die where he was found. There's no way.'

Although he still thinks the case is really mysterious, Alan doesn't think UFOs were involved in Zyggy's death. Which gives more credence to his own encounter.

He tells us about that night and how he came across the UFO. I ask him how much time he reckons he lost, and Alan says, 'Between about ten past five in the morning and ten to six.' So that's about forty minutes that he can't account for.

He draws me and Travis an image of what the UFO looked like – a flying saucer, with panels underneath and fairground-type lights round the outside. Travis says it's very similar to the craft he saw. Old Alan had a framed, hand-drawn picture of a UFO on his kitchen wall as well.

Alan describes the creatures he saw as having a head like a light bulb and a child-like body, which has become a popular image of aliens more recently but it wasn't back then. Back in the seventies the little green man was more popular, rather than the 'greys' that Alan has just described.

Alan also tells us about going into regression with a police psychiatrist. He had been pretty sceptical about it, and when he watched the tape back, it shit him up. He says it wasn't him, by which he means it felt as if he was watching someone else going through the experience.

Alan seems pretty credible to me. Again, I don't want to come across like I just swallow anything UFO-related – I try to judge each case on its own merits and each person on their own merits. Obviously, when someone's telling you a story about what happened to them, you're judging them, both consciously and subconsciously – not just what they're saying, but how they're saying it, their actions and all sorts. You do that with anyone you just met, don't you? It's human nature. And what I see makes me believe him.

Alan then agrees to take us to where the incident happened, by the police station. By this time it's dark, and we can get a sense of what it must have been like that night. Although Alan was on his own when he saw the craft, there were several other spottings that night. One major detail that backs up Alan's story is that other cops also saw something that matched Alan's description of the UFO, and they filed reports independently.

'Twelve miles away from where I was, three police officers got up on t'moor, and as they're driving up there, they became aware of this blue pulsating light in the sky, on the horizon. They stood watching this object, and then – sssssshhhhoooommmm – it went from one side of the horizon to t'other, in a split second, it went backwards and forwards, up and down . . . and they then observed it heading in the general direction of Todmorden.'

Two other coppers in the Todmorden area also saw a

craft and submitted a report with their own drawing of it, which was very similar to Alan's drawing.

I do disagree with Alan on one thing though. He thinks the two incidents were unrelated, that it was just coincidence that they both happened to him but I don't really believe in coincidence, so I'm not having that. As far as I'm concerned, if those two incidents happened to Alan, and I believe that they did, then they're definitely connected.

After we leave Alan, me and Travis go for a drink to have a chat. Travis reckons Alan has three things in his favour – he was a police officer, he had the corroboration of other police officers who saw the same thing, and as a police officer he had a lot at stake by coming out and being public about what had happened. Some of his superiors even advised him not to say anything and tried to shush him up. You can see why the Old Bill in some small town wouldn't want one of their cops going round spouting off about how he'd seen a UFO. Especially in the seventies. You've got all the locals, who are probably a bit straight, thinking, 'We can't have this guy as our cop, he sounds a bit unstable', you know what I mean? I can see why it wouldn't look good. Alan even said he had other coppers try and plant stuff in his locker to try and discredit him.

Travis says he was impressed by Alan's own astonishment at his regression, and thinks that counts in his favour. Travis also knows about a case involving a cop in New Mexico that sounded pretty similar.

It's hard to know exactly what to make of the incidents in Todmorden but Travis and I are both in agreement that something definitely happened to Alan.

★

That night we drive down south, heading for Suffolk on the next leg of our UFO road trip. We are heading to Suffolk to investigate the Rendlesham Forest incident.

I already know a lot about this case, as I've seen it on various documentaries over the years. It happened just outside RAF Woodbridge and RAF Bentwaters Air Force bases in late December 1980, which at the time were both used by the US Air Force, so most of the witnesses were Yanks. Dozens of USAF personnel were involved in various incidents on the base after going into the forest to investigate mysterious lights. What happened next has been debated for over thirty years, and is still being debated today. Even those who were there can't agree on what happened, but some of the men have since said they saw an alien spacecraft and at least one of them claimed to have touched it.

Shaun's X-Files

The Rendlesham incident from 1980 has been dubbed 'the British Roswell' by many people. Some files released by the National Archives show that Rendlesham remains the UK's most enduringly fascinating UFO sighting. Dr David Clarke, who analysed all the documents released by the National Archives, estimated that 'almost half' of all UFO correspondence directed at defence officials related to requests for information or 'tip-offs' about the Rendlesham incident. Dr Clarke came to the conclusion that, 'There is no way you will be able to get to the truth of what happened because like a snowball rolling down the hill, the stories have been more and more embellished.'

The incident started around 3 a.m. on Boxing Day 1980 when strange lights were reported descending into the forest. At first, the Air Force dudes who saw the lights thought a plane had come down, but when they went into the forest to investigate they witnessed a 'strange, glowing object, metallic in appearance, with coloured lights'. One of the American geezers, Sgt James Penniston, later described it as a 'craft of unknown origin' and claimed he touched the craft and it was 'warm'. He also described symbols on the exterior of the craft, which he copied down. The local police were called but the only light they could see was the one from Orford Ness lighthouse, which was a few miles away on the coast (well, obviously it was on the coast – where else are you going to have a lighthouse?).

Unlike most cases, which involve a single sighting and last a matter of minutes, this incident was stretched over several days.

The next morning after the first sighting, the same

guys returned to the clearing in the forest where it had happened, and found three triangular impressions in the ground and burn marks on the trees.

From everything I've seen and read before today, it seems to me that something *definitely* went down that night at that military base. The other thing that is interesting is that there are theories that some bods high up in the military knew what was going on that night, almost as if it was a prearranged meeting with aliens or something. Or as if it was a set-up and they wanted to monitor reactions. I don't quite know, but there is definitely more than meets the eye to the story, and there's definitely some withholding of information going on. Someone, and probably quite a few people, knew more than they were letting on about what happened that night, and they still haven't come clean, so I'm keen to try and get to the bottom of it.

We'd arranged to meet one of the original witnesses, called Larry Warren, in a country pub near where the incident happened. It feels a bit like the three amigos with me, Larry and Travis all having had a life-changing UFO adventure. Larry and Travis had met each other a few times before at UFO conferences, which is hardly surprising since they're two of the most in-demand dudes in the UFO world. Larry's a character. He seems to be happy to be out with the boys – the first thing he says to me is 'Shaun! How you doing, brother?'

Larry acts as if me, him and Travis are old school mates who haven't seen each other in years, finally getting the old band together. It's quite amusing and endearing. He has a goatee beard and is going grey, and looks like he's done his share of partying over the years. He also has a gravelly voice which sounds like it has paid the price for some of that partying. 'It almost looks like Shaun Ryder and Travis Walton meets Willie Nelson,' he rasps, 'the way I'm looking right now with the beard and all.'

Larry says to me, 'I remember when you guys were hitting NYC in the nineties and the whole Manchester scene was kicking off, that was great. Man, it's a weird life we lead.'

You can say that again. The last month or so has been one of the weirdest trips of my life.

While we're waiting for the crew to set up, Larry asks Travis something about his movie. 'You know my favourite part of the movie, Travis – and I know you know I've watched it loads and it's one of my favourite films – my favourite part is when you're sat in your truck in town, and the little kid comes up to you and says. "Can I have your autograph?" and you say "Why?" and the kid says, "You've been to space."'

'Well, I'll tell you what really happened,' says Travis, 'which is that I was on set during the filming of the movie, and this kid was running round getting all the autographs of all the actors and he said to me, "Hey, are you famous? Can I have your autograph?" I'm not sure he knew who I was.'

It seems like Larry and Travis are treated like pop stars when they turn up at UFO conferences because their experiences are so famous. They talk about some of the other well-known characters that they both know on the UFO scene. It sounds a bit like when you're in a band and you're doing the summer festival circuit, and you end up bumping into the same bands backstage at different festivals. 'All right, how's it going? What time you on today? Have a good one . . .'

'I've been back to Missouri a few times this year. I did a thing with Peter in Maine and we had to share a room,' says Travis. 'Never share a room with Peter, I gotta tell you he snores a whole bunch for a small guy.'

In December 1980, Larry was a fresh-faced recruit based at RAF Bentwaters. He was dragged into the Rendlesham Forest incident on the third night and has a lot to say about it. When he was honourably discharged from the United States Air Force in 1983, he went public with his version of what happened. He's spent the last thirty years defying the authorities to tell his story.

Like I said, I've heard a lot about this story over the years, so I tell Larry I've always wanted to hear it from the horse's mouth. 'Well, I'll tell it, brother,' he rasps.

'It was a clear night. I didn't know the area that well. We got to a clearing called Cable Green and there was a mist or a fog that was greenish yellow, on the ground, in a circular shape. The air was charged, yet movement was slow and there was no sound. Everything was void, it was like a vacuum.'

Larry then describes a red ball of light that appeared

and moved into the clearing, which is a description that has been substantiated by other accounts of that night.

'By the time my eyes cleared there was a structured object, about thirty feet at its base and it went up to a point, like a pyramid. I was about twenty feet away and I saw these life forms ... I thought they looked like kids, and I was like, 'What *is this?*' ... it was animated and it was alive.'

Larry admits himself that his account is a bit dreamlike. But he says that this haziness was due to some sort of force field that was coming from the structure.

What is definite though — and Larry stills seems pissed off, rightly if you ask me — is that after he stood guard for a while, as other officers took radiation readings, he and other low-ranking officers were ordered back to base, while the mysterious objects were still there in the field. I ask him what explanation his superiors gave him.

'They didn't tell us it was from outer space but they definitely told us that this phenomenon had been visiting this planet for longer than any of us in the room could appreciate. They said they hoped we appreciated the need for secrecy and hoped they could count on our cooperation.'

'Cooperation meaning don't talk about it?' asks Travis.

'Don't talk about it,' says Larry, nodding. 'They had us sign pre-prepared witness statements saying that we were off duty and saw lights in the trees.'

He adds, 'The real twisted part with this is . . . hey, I always say "twisting" with you, Shaun. Why is that?' He's a bit of a comedian, Larry.

'Dunno, Larry,' I reply. 'Something to do with my melons?'

I tell Larry that I actually nicked the phrase 'twisting my melon' off Steve McQueen for 'Step On'. It surprises me how many people don't know 'Step On' is a cover version, although the Happy Mondays version is now much more well-known than the sixties original. It all came about when we were asked to do a cover version for our American label, Elektra, for their fortieth anniversary. They wanted all their bands to cover something else on the label so they sent us a tape of Elektra songs to consider and the first or second song on there was 'Step On' by John Kongos. I'd never heard it before but I liked it and I could tell it would be an easy one for us to rip and make our own, which is what we did. It became almost a completely different track by the time we'd finished with it, and then Paul Oakenfold had put his stamp on it.

As I told Larry, the 'twisting my melon' bit came from Steve McQueen. In a roundabout way. I'd been watching this Steve McQueen documentary called *Man on the Edge* because I was bang into him. In the documentary, one of the big producers from Fox or one of the other big film studios was describing how he first met McQueen and says something like, 'This cool kid came in, and you could tell he was an actor. He looked like a cool street kid and he said to me, "You can't tell me what's what man! You're twisting my melon man!"' That's what McQueen was like, an uncompromising little fucker. Can you imagine One Direction or someone saying something like that?

This producer carried on, 'This kid spoke so hip, he didn't know what he was saying!' Straightaway, while I was watching it, I thought, 'I'll have that, thank you very much' – 'You're twisting my melon man, you know you talk so hip, you're twisting my melon man.' I knew that's what was needed for 'Step On': a killer catchphrase.

I always thought McQueen was a cool fucker. I actually got into him before I found out about his background. He had been an orphan as a kid and then he joined the Marines. He got into acting because he realized it was full of birds, and posh birds at that. Which was great by me. All I knew about him at first was that he had a great haircut and wore really cool clothes, and not much else matters to you at that age. It makes me laugh when people wank on about James Dean being the coolest guy that ever lived. *Please.* James Dean? He wasn't even in the same league as Steve McQueen.

The other catchphrase in 'Step On' was the 'Call the cops!' line. That one came from a pal of ours in the Hacienda called Bobby Gillette, who was always shouting, 'Call the cops!' He'd stand in the Hacienda, off his nut, whistling and shouting, 'Call the cops! . . . We're here! The Mancs! Our firm! Our corner! . . . CALL THE COPS!' So I just stuck those two elements together and came up with: 'You're twisting my melon man, you talk so hip, you know you're twisting my melon man . . . call the cops!' and it worked great on our version of 'Step On'. That line has stuck with me over the years, so much so that I decided to call my autobiography *Twisting My*

Melon when I wrote it a couple of years ago. I quite like the fact that no one knows what it means, but everyone has their own take on it.

Anyway, getting back to old Larry and him getting his melons twisted in Rendlesham Forest. Over the years a number of men have come forward with their versions of what happened during the Rendlesham incident, and I have to say some of their accounts differ quite a lot. But there is also a radio recording of what happened that night, which seems to suggest they definitely saw a UFO. Larry says he'll drive us out to show us the area where the incident happened.

Larry still finds it quite traumatic being at the site, even after all these years. 'I never wanted to come back here. I thought it was pretty evil. Not in a satanic way, but just . . . my world became totally different that night.'

Some of the people who were with Larry that night definitely think evil was involved. I do find that is the natural reaction of some people when they're confronted with something that they can't comprehend or understand. They panic and think it's the devil's work. Rather than thinking it might be a good thing, they naturally assume the worst.

'To me, as a young man,' says Larry, 'it just spun the world that I thought I knew upside down.'

I ask him what is his own personal take on what happened that night.

'My personal belief, thirty-two years later, is that they [the Air Force and other authorities] had equipment preset up here that was designed to bring in phenomena and other intelligence. Their plan was to contain this phenomenon and observe it under close quarters, with the Special Forces they had set up around the forest.'

'So you believe they attracted these visitors?' I ask.

'I believe they, the government, the Feds, whoever, had the technology, which is beyond me, that could open the door to this phenomenon, so they could observe it. But this thing got out of hand. Maybe it was only supposed to be one night, but it turned into three, and I think they pissed this phenomenon off. That's why it got too big and beings were coming down here.'

Larry also reckoned the authorities had nuclear power present.

'The nuclear power that we had was adversely affected by the phenomenon.'

Something truly weird obviously happened that night in Rendlesham. But I find it hard to separate the fact from fiction, even with Larry. I like Larry, but he's quite angry. He seems to be angry with the world, that this happened to him, and more than that, the way it had happened. There were two guys who, years later, had come out with their own version of the story, and he is particularly angry with them: 'Why did they not say this at the time?' They didn't say anything for years and all of a sudden, twenty-five years later, they came out and said, 'We touched the craft, and we got something, and they were time travellers.'

But if these guys did keep quiet for ages, I can see they

might do that because they were career military dudes, you know what I mean? Their dads were in the Air Force. Their dads' dads were in the Air Force. It was a career for them. They weren't just some guys who signed up to get the fuck out of Hicksville USA. They were from military families whose whole lives going back generations were based around the military. So it made total sense to me that they didn't want to come out and talk about it. They were just closing ranks. That's what the military does, isn't it? Literally. You don't shit on your own.

'You know what it's like, Travis,' Larry says. 'I know you've had people questioning what you say, and I know your head spins with it, or used to.'

Larry actually thinks he was lucky not to get whacked because he wouldn't shut up about the incident. And do you know what? Maybe he's right. I know that sounds a bit *Goodfellas*, but the authorities were trying to shush him up for a long time. There were plenty of people back in the day who were linked to stories that were sensitive to governments and then happened to meet with 'unfortunate accidents'. I think that sort of thing is less likely to happen nowadays, partly because it would be harder to cover up.

But make no mistake; governments don't like you going round talking about something that they want to keep quiet.

Especially the US government.

CHAPTER 11

Meeting the Pope

AS I MENTIONED earlier, I wanted to meet as many credible figures as possible during my mission, and Nick Pope was exactly the sort of geezer that I wanted to talk to. I've always had a bit of an issue with the way UFO witnesses are judged – the credibility of a sighting seems to depend on who sees it. If you or I spot a UFO, it's unlikely many people will believe us, but it's a different matter if it's a large group of individuals working within the military or government. That makes even the sceptics sit up and take notice.

Nick Pope is a very interesting dude because he's a former member of the Ministry of Defence whose opinions on UFOs are taken very seriously indeed. I've seen him on TV over the years and read his book, and what I like about Nick is he isn't *supposed* to believe. He first joined the MOD in 1985, and did a few different jobs before 1991 when he was appointed to Secretariat (Air Staff) Department 2A – which is a right mouthful, but basically to those in the know at the MOD, it was the 'UFO desk'. His job was to investigate and analyse claims of UFO sightings and to assess their threat to national security. Little did he know that the job was going to change his life.

It's pretty obvious to me that he was chosen for the job because he was a safe bet. He was from a military background and his dad was in the secret service. It counts in your favour, doesn't it, if you come from a military background and you're almost conditioned to it from birth? He was also a UFO sceptic, which helped. Obviously they didn't want to put some absolute UFO nut in the MOD job, giving them access to all sorts of secret files. So when the job came up, someone obviously went, 'What about young Nick Pope . . . Popey's boy? Let's get him in. He doesn't believe in all this stuff and he's only twenty-one, he's not going to go out and start mouthing off and causing us problems. He's perfect. Give Popey's lad a shout . . .'

So Popey's lad gets the gig because he's one of their own, you know what I mean? He's family, and he doesn't really believe in all this stuff. And when Nick comes in on his first day, he has the attitude that it's pretty much all bullshit. But then over the first year or two of the gig, he starts seeing all this evidence come across his desk that can't just be explained away, and he's like, 'Whoa, hang on a minute, there's actually some weird shit going on here.'

Apparently some ufologists like Doug Cooper were happy to work with him and talk to him as part of official investigations. But some other ufologists saw him as 'a sinister *Man in Black* type character' and refused to have anything to do with him, as they believed the MOD and its staff were all part of a conspiracy to cover up the truth about UFOs.

At the time, the MOD stated in public that it 'remains totally open-minded about the existence or otherwise of extraterrestrial life forms', but the staff reckoned there was no evidence to suggest that any UFO sightings posed any threat to the UK or that they were extraterrestrial. Nick clearly didn't agree that all the UFO sightings he came across could be explained away that easily. He resigned from the MOD in 2006, saying the government's 'X-Files have been closed down', and in 2009 the MOD announced that UFO sightings would no longer be investigated. By then Nick had already started giving interviews to the press about it all and speaking pretty openly about it. From starting out as a sceptic, he had become a firm believer in UFOs.

For instance, on 9 November 2006 the *Evening Standard* newspaper ran an article under the headline '"Aliens could attack at any time" warns former MOD chief'. Nick Pope is quoted as saying that 'highly credible' sightings of UFO activity were just being dismissed by the MOD and the effective closure of the UFO desk was leaving the county wide open for extraterrestrial interference. 'The consequences of getting this one wrong could be huge,' he said, even though he believed that as yet there was no evidence of a hostile threat.

In the article he acknowledges that reports such as a 1993 sighting of a 'vast, triangular-shaped craft' over Air Force bases in the West Midlands had convinced him that there was something out there that needed investigating. He also mentioned the Rendlesham incident in 1980.

Since leaving the MOD, Nick Pope has continued to investigate UFO sightings and has become one of the world's leading experts. He's also published a bestselling book called *Open Skies, Open Minds – For the first time a government UFO expert speaks out.*

Nick has agreed to meet up with me and suggests taking me to the National Archives to go over some of the most interesting UFO files there. I've seen the National Archives before on documentaries and I've always fancied having a poke around in there. Who wouldn't? So it sounds like a great plan to me.

We meet first for a brew in a posh little café in Kew, in West London, which is a bit fancy. I like Nick straightaway. I think he is a totally straight-up dude. You can tell that common sense had just prevailed with him. I find it hard to believe that some ufologists wouldn't deal with him because they thought he was some shady *Men in Black* dude. He's just a normal guy, he's hardly Tommy Lee Smith, you know what I mean? The first thing I want to ask Nick is what his feelings were about UFOs before he got the job.

'When I started that job I was broadly sceptical,' he explains. 'I really didn't know much about the subject. When I came out of the job after three years I had changed my mind. While I'm not a total believer, I certainly know that there's more to this than misidentification or hoaxes, there's something weird going on in our skies.'

I ask him if he thinks governments take UFOs seriously.

'Yes, they do. This is a serious issue. If there is anything unknown in your airspace, particularly if it's been seen by pilots and tracked on radar, then the military and governments want to know what it is, so it doesn't surprise me that governments all over the world have UFO departments.'

I tell him about my first encounters that I had when I was a kid back in the seventies, and he says there was a huge spike in the amount of reports of UFOs to the MOD during that decade. I'm also intrigued to find out what was the most interesting case he came across while he was in the job on the UFO desk.

'The most fascinating case I came across when I was running the UFO desk was the Cosford incident in 1993, when there was a wave of incidents over a few hours, including sightings at two military bases. There were lots of reports from military personnel and police. I spoke to the Met Officer at RAF Shawbury, the morning after, and his voice was shaking as he told me about a huge diamond-shaped UFO.'

The Met Officer described to Nick how it had moved slowly across the countryside towards the base at a speed of no more than 30 or 40 mph. He saw the UFO fire a narrow beam of light, a bit like a laser, at the ground and then saw the light sweeping backwards and forwards across the field, as if it were looking for something. It sounds like a searchlight that you see on prison watchtowers in the movies. He heard an unpleasant low-frequency humming sound coming from the craft and said he could feel as well as hear it – rather like standing in front of a bass speaker. I'm not sure if the 'bass speaker' part of the story was the Met Officer or Nick Pope's description. It made me wonder if one of them was an old raver. I couldn't really picture Nick on the dancefloor at the Hacienda, but you never know! He might have thrown some shapes in his time.

I'd heard about the Costord case before and I am keen to know more about it. Nick had made a programme about it for Channel 5 in 2006, which was based on the original MOD files and was a pretty decent show for that channel, to be fair. Obviously the fact that a lot of the witnesses were officials and police made it a lot more credible in some people's eyes. Nick says there's a lot of info on the case in the National Archives, which holds copies of all the UFO reports ever filed and he says he'll take me there now and show me, which is music to my ears. I can't wait to get my mitts on some proper official reports. I feel like a proper investigator.

Shaun's X-Files

The National Archives is the archive of the UK government and it holds over 1,000 years of the nation's records for everyone to discover and use. The National Archives' collection of over eleven million historical government and public records is one of the largest in the world. It includes everything from the Domesday Book to modern government papers and digital files, electronic records, photographs, posters, maps, drawings and paintings.

When we get to the National Archives, Nick clearly knows his way round the place, which is great. It's like having my own private expert guide to the nation's UFO files, which is ace. It's kind of pretty much what you'd imagine the National Archives to be like, just rows and rows of shelves full of files, like a massive, fuck-off library. When we get to the UFO section it makes me laugh that a load of the files have a big 'X' on the side. 'Are these the real life X-Files, then?' I joke with Nick.

A lot of the stuff here is open to the general public for viewing, but not everything. Nick explains that some files that are now a hundred years old are still closed. What secrets are so dangerous that you can't let the public know about them a century later? 'What's in those files?' I joke with Nick. 'Was Jack the Ripper actually a member of the Royal Family or something?'

When we're looking at the files and handling them, we have to wear little white gloves. I feel like Minnie bloody Mouse or one of those mime artists.

The first files we look at are those on the Cosford incident, which happened on the night of 30 March 1993 and involved hundreds of witnesses. The episode began with two reported sightings in Somerset. The first witness was a copper who described seeing a craft that looked like two Concordes flying side by side. A group of Scouts had also seen the same thing. Later that same night, 200 miles north of the Somerset sightings, officers at RAF Cosford and RAF Shawbury reported seeing similar craft flying over their military bases. The fact that loads of military officers reported it obviously made people sit up and pay attention.

Nick was in his job at the time at the MOD so all the reports of such incidents landed on his desk. By the time he got to work in the morning there was a bunch of reports already waiting for him.

Shaun's X-Files

The 1993 Cosford incident is one of the UK's biggest unexplained UFO cases to date.

Unlike many UFO stories, the core collection of sightings – timed between 1.10 a.m. and 1.15 a.m. – tallied to a remarkable degree. Most described two bright white lights speeding towards the south-east horizon, leaving trails of luminous vapour in their wake.

Nick pulls out a map that he drew at the time, plotting all the various sightings connected to the Cosford incident. There was a whole bunch of reports from various witnesses. Nick showed me one from the Met Officer at RAF Cosford and his description of the way the craft crossed the sky reminds me of my own encounter back in the seventies.

Checks that were done at the time ruled out the possibility that it could have been military or civilian aircraft. Radar records were carefully scrutinized but they all drew a blank. As a result Pope cited this case as the turning point on his tour of duty – the 'big case' that led him to believe that extraterrestrials really were able to penetrate Britain's defences at will.

RAF Fylingdales – an early warning station in North Yorkshire that tracks satellites and ballistic missiles – told Nick that a Russian rocket had re-entered the atmosphere around the same time. But Nick didn't accept that and wrote to DI55, the branch of the defence intelligence staff who handle this sort of sighting, telling them: 'Whilst the decay . . . might explain some of the high altitude sightings, it does not explain the low level sightings. It also fails to explain [the] report of a low hum, or the report from Mr Elliott, the Met Officer at RAF Shawbury. The spread of timings and bearings of the sightings also argues against this decay explaining all of them.'

I ask Nick what he reckoned happened that night.

'I don't know. To this day the whole incident is completely unexplained.'

He's a clever bloke Nick, so although he's very open-minded, he's not going to come out and say it was definitely a UFO or make wild suggestions without proper proof. He then shows me what he calls the 'killer document' on the case. It's from the Ministry of Defence and says, 'in summary, there would seem to be some evidence on this occasion that an unidentified object or objects of unknown origin, was operating above the UK'.

That is an official report from the MOD almost admitting that they reckon there was an UFO in our skies that night. Nick agrees with me. 'That's an absolute fantastic line. It's the nearest the MOD has ever come to saying UFOs are real, they're in our airspace, but we don't know what they are.'

Bloody hell. I don't think that line has been reported as much as it should have been. I'd never heard that from the MOD before. It was well worth coming to the National Archives just to have that one line from the MOD.

I read it again to myself: 'there would seem to be some evidence on this occasion that an unidentified object or objects of unknown origin, was operating above the UK'.

You're not going to get more than that from the bloody

MOD are you? That's only one step away from saying, 'Guess what, folks? UFOs are real and they're here.'

Shaun's X-Files

In 2012, nearly 7,000 previously secret documents detailing UFO sightings were released by the MOD. Access to these official papers is encouraging for people who believe they've encountered or even communicated with extraterrestrials. The documents were released after a campaign by Dr David Clarke, who had been asking the Ministry of Defence to release the files since 2003.

Among the 7,000 files were documents detailing that:

- Tony Blair was briefed on UFO and alien defence policy as he was so concerned about the disclosure of classified information on extraterrestrials when he was Prime Minister;
- a Whitehall civil servant was paid to investigate UFO reports;
- government officials believed aliens might be space tourists and suggested harnessing UFO technology for British defences.

One of the most interesting files that the MOD released in 2003 related to an MOD officer. It doesn't give his name in the file, but the officer claims that aliens might 'come here for holidays'. Which made me laugh.

Earth can't be all that bad, can it, if aliens who have the ability to travel through space and visit different planets were choosing to come here for the holidays? Can you imagine an alien couple on their spaceship, debating where they're going to go this year? He's saying, 'What about that new moon that's just been discovered in Andromeda II galaxy? That looks pretty interesting.' And she's giving it, 'Can we just go back to Earth again, it's really pretty.' He'd probably warn her that they were in danger of getting spotted if they kept coming back, but she'd still get her own way.

In the file, which dates from 1995, the desk officer said he thought we really needed to work out why UFOs were coming here and it was 'essential that we start with open minds . . . what is scientific "fact" today may not be true tomorrow'.

While he made it clear he didn't 'talk to little green men every night', he also said, 'We have a remit that we have never satisfied. That is, we do not know if UFOs exist . . . If they do exist, we do not know what they are, their purpose or if they pose a threat to the UK . . . if the sightings are of devices not of the Earth then their purpose needs to be established as a matter of priority. There has been no apparent hostile intent and other possibilities are: 1) Military reconnaissance; 2) Scientific; 3) Tourism.'

There was another file from 1979, but the author found it a bit harder to believe aliens would come here by choice for their holidays. The document, which had

175

been prepared for a House of Lords debate into UFOs, wondered why aliens would want to visit 'an insignificant planet (the Earth) of an uninteresting star (the sun)'. But you can't prejudge where people might go for their holidays, can you? I wonder why people would go on holiday to an 'insignificant' place like Bognor Regis, but they still do.

A separate file released at the same time by the MOD revealed that Tony Blair had requested information about UFOs after he came into office in 1998. The MOD sent him a long reply, explaining that the ministry 'has only a limited interest in UFO matters' but that they 'remain open minded' about the existence of 'extraterrestrial life forms'.

But Tony Blair was not the only British Prime Minister who wanted to find out more about UFOs. Nick pulls out another file to show me, which includes a note from Winston Churchill asking the MOD to tell him more.

'What does all this stuff about flying saucers amount to?' wrote Churchill. 'What can it mean? What is the truth? Let me have a full report at your convenience.'

There is also a file in which a scientist who said his grandfather was one of Churchill's bodyguards accused Churchill of covering up a close encounter between an RAF aircraft and a UFO during the Second World War. This scientist explained how his grandfather, who served with the RAF in the war, was present when Churchill and US General Dwight D. Eisenhower discussed how to deal with the UFO encounter.

The man, who is not named in the files, said Churchill was reported to have exclaimed: 'This event should be immediately classified since it would create mass panic amongst the general population and destroy one's belief in the church.'

When some other geezer who was in the meeting said he thought it was a UFO, Churchill declared that the incident should be classified 'for at least 50 years and its status reviewed by a future Prime Minister'. Which is why we've only just found out about it now, sixty years later. Makes you wonder what has happened more recently but won't be announced until another fifty or sixty years have gone.

There's also a file in the National Archives about some geezer from Leeds who had put a bet on at Ladbrokes in 1990 on whether alien life would be discovered before the end of the century. The actual betting slip says, 'Aliens to have landed (dead or alive) on Earth before 31 December 1999'. Ladbrokes gave him 100–1 and he stuck £3 on it. Apparently the geezer was pissed off because he reckoned that he had won his bet, but Ladbrokes wouldn't pay out because the United Nations had not confirmed the existence of aliens. I saw he had another bet on the same slip – he'd stuck £2 on Germany to win the 1990 World Cup, so at least he made his money back!

Spending a day with Nick going through the files at the National Archives has been fascinating. There is evidence from a lot of credible witnesses, including police officers, military police and members of the Air

Force, not just fruitcakes or bubblegum heads. The vast quantity of UFO reports in the National Archives prove that many people in the UK believe they exist.

For someone like me who is fascinated by UFOs, it makes me feel reassured that I'm not alone in this world.

In more ways than one.

CHAPTER 12

The Church of UFOs

AFTER SPENDING SOME time with Nick Pope at the National Archives, I begin to think about how UFO witnesses in this country are treated. When UFO stories are covered in the media, they're more often than not the jokey item at the end of the news, despite the fact that large numbers of the population believe they exist. Perhaps that is one reason why there are specialist UFO groups and societies. It must be hard if you've had an experience but people around you don't believe a word you're saying – no wonder you'd go looking for people who had had similar experiences.

The next day I meet with a former clinical psychologist, Dr Peter McCue, who I mentioned earlier. He worked for many years as a clinical psychologist in the NHS, and has a longstanding interest in psychical research and ufology. I want to learn more about his take on why people join these groups and whether or not they help validate UFO sightings. Peter seems a bit wary of some of these groups.

'I suppose if people believe and have a certain belief they might want to recruit to make other people share that belief. It makes them feel better and there may be processes within the group where someone becomes a kind of guru figure, and if they're believed then other people will follow that. I think that sort of activity is one that can bring the whole subject into doubt in other people's minds.'

I can see Peter's point – some UFO groups can be seen as a bit wacky, but I want to check one of them out for myself.

After doing some research, me and the team decide to check out the UFO Academy, which is based in a gaff called High Elms Manor in Hertfordshire, just outside Watford. High Elms Manor is a Grade II listed Georgian house, which is owned by Sheila O'Neill and the UFO Academy is run by her daughter Catrine and Catrine's partner Edwin. It's a group for people who want to share their experiences and 'investigate all aspects including the spiritual connection'.

It's a lovely gaff and Catrine is really welcoming to me, but after that nice introduction the evening starts to go downhill as far as I'm concerned. I'm sitting there in this group of people for about three hours in total, but it feels a lot, lot longer. Almost as soon as the evening starts,

I'm actually a little shocked about how amateur it all is. I don't want to be rude to anyone, but the majority of stuff that the group presents to us about their experiences is just so . . . small time. It's just really bog-standard stuff that might have impressed people in the fifties, but not in this day and age. At one point someone gets up and shows the whole room a projection of a picture they took, which looks to me like a Reni hat – you know the kind of hats that Reni from the Stone Roses wears? – and claims it's a bloody UFO. I'm like, 'Really? Come on, man!' I'm sorry, but I'm really just not impressed at all.

Someone gets up at one point and starts talking quite happily about how they have been abducted by aliens and all about the experience. Now, I'm sorry, but I don't think you would be that happy about being abducted if you had been. The people who are believable to me are the ones who say they have been abducted but are obviously still traumatized by it. The ones who look like they have just come back from Beirut, Vietnam, Northern Ireland and the Normandy landings all rolled into one. The people here look like they have just come back off holiday.

I'm not having it. But most of the congregation are lapping it up. It feels more like a group therapy session than an investigation into the paranormal, it really does. At one stage one of the speakers says, 'Make it normal, make it real, speak from your heart . . .'

At the end of the evening, I just feel like all these people might have slightly empty lives and are looking for something to believe in, and for someone to believe them. I almost feel they believe it more than Catrine and Edwin who run the gaff. I think it's good that there is a community for believers, but it's not for me.

★

After my experience at the UFO society, we decide to delve a bit deeper into the spiritual side of ufology, which is all new to me. I don't really have any other beliefs apart from UFOs, so there's no real spiritual slant to my own personal belief in UFOs. But I'm about to find out a bit more about those people who mix religion and the extraterrestrial.

I'm visiting a worldwide organization called the Aetherius Society at their headquarters in London. It was started back in the fifties by people who believe that contacting extraterrestrials is the key to healing humanity and restoring balance on planet Earth. They also combine their beliefs in UFOs with bits that they nick like a magpie from other religions, as well as a bit of yoga. I'm sure it won't surprise you that I'm not exactly a massive yoga nut. The only geezer from round our way who's into yoga is Ryan Giggs, who lives just round the corner. Mind you, it's done him all right with the football, he's about sixty-three now and he's still playing for Man United.

After my last group experience at the UFO Academy, I'm feeling a bit apprehensive. Especially as I've read up a bit more about the Aetherius Society on their website, which explains how they believe they are 'cooperating with the Gods from Space'. I don't want to start prejudging anyone, but when someone tells me they're 'cooperating with the Gods from Space', then forgive me if a little alarm bell starts ringing.

Shaun's X-Files

The Aetherius Society is a UFO religion founded by George King in the 1950s, which combines belief in UFOs with yoga and ideas from various religions like Hinduism, Buddhism, Christianity and Theosophy. The society was set up by King after a voice said to him, 'Prepare yourself! You are to become the voice of Interplanetary Parliament.'

Its goal is 'to prevent the annihilation of the Earth by improving cooperation between humanity and various alien species, and by improving the spiritual lives of the world'. The society claims that various disasters may be prevented by prayer, often aided by 'Spiritual Energy Batteries' that store healing psychic energy.

The members are preparing for the 'Next Master', a messianic figure who they believe will descend to Earth in a flying saucer. The society is named after Aetherius – King said he was in telepathic contact with this being who is believed to be a 'Cosmic Master' from Venus, along with Buddha and Jesus.

One of the first things I notice on my visit is that there seems to be quite a lot of money pouring into the place, with Bentleys and Mercs parked outside – I don't think many of the members had taken two buses to get there, put it that way. The headquarters is in a pretty respectable area and the people I meet there have good jobs – company directors and what have you. It does make me think that perhaps it is no coincidence that the Aetherius Society is located here, in a leafy party of posh London, rather than in Burnley or Doncaster, you know what I mean?

I meet Richard Lawrence, who is the Executive Secretary of the Aetherius Society for Europe, and a Bishop in the Aetherius Churches. He's a really nice bloke, and we have a good conversation, with him explaining the background of the society and me letting him know where I'm coming from. He doesn't even get the hump when I rib him a bit about some of the more far-out elements of their beliefs. He's done loads of TV and radio over the years, everything from GMTV to LBC, and had a column in the *Observer* newspaper. He discovered the Aetherius Society in 1971 when he was a student at Hull University, and he found that it answered a lot of his questions, so he got more and more interested in it.

Tonight, I'm here to sit in on their two-hour service or prayer meeting, and I appreciate them letting me do that because it's quite a private thing, isn't it?

If I thought the UFO Academy was slightly weird, then the Aetherius Society is next-level stuff. At one stage they all start chanting a mantra, 'ommmm, titty, titty, ommmmmm, titty'. I'm not being funny, it's hard work. Sitting there for two hours chanting the mantra and everything is enough to make you lightheaded and dizzy.

Towards the end they're all praying to a box and the spiritual energy inside it, or the 'Spiritual Energy Battery' as they call it. Basically, as far as I can work out, they're all channelling their energy into this box, which they then send out to the universe. I mention to Richard that I'm not sure about the whole putting-energy-inside-a-box thing and that it all seems a bit farfetched.

He says, 'It *is* different, I admit, and I don't really expect you to take my word for it, I just invite you to see what we do. We discharge this, as we call it, in cooperation with beings from other planets, and we keep a log of the discharges and where it goes to and when, and we see what the effects are over a period of time.'

It's exactly the sort of stuff that Louis Theroux would lap up, you know what I mean? He'd play along and be really dry through it all, like he was smarter than them. As I've said, I'd rather not do that. I don't want to just rip the piss out of people's beliefs, but I'm just not buying this lot at all. To be honest, this is not exactly the type of ufology I was mad keen on exploring for this book and my TV show, but I suppose you've got to look at all avenues, haven't you?

Richard and the people in the Aetherius Society obviously believe it and at the end of the day, is there much difference between praying to a Spiritual Energy

Battery and praying to a tabernacle in a Catholic church? Catholics reckon that Christ is in the tabernacle, so these Aetherius dudes believing that energy and all their prayers are in a box is not that different. My vibe is that if they believe it – and I can tell by the look in the eyes of some of the congregation that they really do believe it – then just leave them to it, let them get on with it. They're not exactly hurting anyone, are they? There are thousands of people in churches across Britain every Sunday morning who are involved in ceremonies that are not too dissimilar. So I'm prepared to try and respect the Aetherius stuff like any other religion or belief. But I won't be back any time soon.

*

The more approaches to ufology that I learn about, the more I wonder about people who believe they've been abducted by aliens. The Ministry of Defence files showed me lots of evidence about people witnessing UFOs. The scientists made me think that one day we may be able to communicate with other civilizations, but actually being abducted is a different matter. I said earlier in the book that the only abductee that I totally believed was Travis Walton but now I'm off to meet Stefan Lobuczek, who says he has been abducted several times. Accounts of abductions like Stefan's are really rare in the UK, so I'm interested in what he has to say. I'm actually pretty jealous. I wouldn't mind having a go at being abducted.

The idea of it frightens me to death, but so does jumping out of a bloody helicopter and I had to do that when I was on *I'm a Celebrity . . . Get Me Out of Here!*

I meet Stefan at his house. He makes me a brew and tells me what happened when he was younger. He started having flashbacks to something he is convinced happened to him when he was a kid. 'I felt this strange sensation and everything seemed to slow down. Almost like a strobe-like flicker. There was this tall thing, which was actually pink in colour.'

I'd read a description where he'd described the alien who was inspecting him as looking like the Pink Panther . . . I ask him whether that's true.

'It sounds really strange, doesn't it? But yes, that's the only thing I could relate it to at the time. I could see like a Perspex cabinet, which was low down and seemed to have chopped off legs in it. Behind me was a cylinder with a severed head in it, and I was thinking, "My God, they're going to take me apart".'

It all sounds pretty bonkers, doesn't it? 'What would you say to people that just say you had a vivid imagination?' I ask Stefan.

'It was real. I can 100 per cent tell you I remember being there. It was *real*. I wouldn't like to be there again.'

Stefan didn't have any explanation as to why the aliens sent some people, like him, back home to Earth, but chopped up other people. Considering what he says happened to him, he didn't seem too much of a nervous wreck about it.

'I deal with it in a different way. I tend to try and have a laugh and a joke about it and that's my way of dealing with it.'

I ask him how he could tell it wasn't just a dream or sleep paralysis or something.

'I'm a very sceptical person. I'm more sceptical about my own experiences than I would be about somebody else's. I've been trying to get to grips with this for years and put it to bed, but it just comes back to haunt me all the time. A lot of people out there could add to what's going on, but they just won't come out because they're frightened of being labelled a nutcase.'

Stefan seems quite sane and rational, despite what he says happened to him. We go outside for a cig and he tells me about an abduction that happened when he went outside for a cig in the middle of the night – a four-foot alien walked through his garden fence and tasered him. Stefan was out cold for a number of hours but he woke up when it was all over.

I've never heard a story as elaborate as Stefan's, and it's hard to take everything on board without evidence. Stefan then offers to take us to his old house where he was abducted as a young boy, aged eleven. He seems pretty relaxed about it all but I know I'd be nervous if I was returning to the spot where a UFO beamed me up.

His account is remarkable but I'm struggling to makes sense of it. I'm hoping this trip will help me sort facts from fantasy.

I ask him how he feels about reliving this stuff.

'I don't like to relive any of it.'

'Would you prefer to knock it on the head and go to the boozer?' I joke.

We then get to the house and it all goes a bit weird. As soon as we get outside the building, Stefan looks more uncomfortable.

'These beings came in the night and they took me, and they took me into a spacecraft and they did things to me, and then they put me back. That happened, from what I remember, twice. I can remember two vivid experiences of being on board some sort of spacecraft.'

'Were you accompanied by an alien?' I ask him.

'There were these two things, short guys, and we travelled up in the light beam together.'

As I quiz him about what happened, Stefan starts freaking out, almost as if he's having a mini panic attack. 'Can we get out of here now? I don't want to be in here any more. Seriously. I don't want to be here any more . . . it's upsetting me.'

He walks off to the car, so I say to the director, 'Look, he's obviously freaked out, so we better do one and get out of here.'

Stefan jumps in the back of the motor, still panicking, and says, 'Let's get the hell out of here . . . quick!'

I try to calm him down, but he's having none of it. 'Just take me home . . . there're just too many memories.'

'Stefan, you'll be fine,' I tell him.

After we've driven a little distance away and he seems

a bit calmed, I ask him, 'Do you ever expect to get any closure on this, Stefan?'

'No, I don't.'

'Do you think this is with you for the rest of your life?'

'Yep, I think it will be.'

Stefan's reaction to the place he believes he was abducted from was shocking and I'm not sure what to make of it. Clearly there has been a chain of events that have deeply affected him, but whether they were extraterrestrial experiences, I'm not too sure. Only Stefan knows the truth.

I'm grateful to Stefan for telling me his story because, from my own experience, I know it can be hard to speak about UFOs when you think people won't believe you. But when I think about what I've learnt from the experts on my journey, I can't help but think there could be other explanations for what happened to Stefan.

★

Even though I wasn't completely convinced by Stefan's account of his abduction, my journey across the UK has generally only strengthened my belief in UFOs. Our researchers were keen for me to meet Dr Lewis Dartnell, who is an astrobiologist at the University of Leicester. He has written a book called *Life in the Universe: A Beginner's Guide*, and also works for *New Scientist* and *Sky at Night*, so he knows his stuff.

He's a nice guy, but he isn't about to let me lure him

into committing to a belief in life out there in space.

'We might receive an unambiguous powerful and intelligent message from a star on the other side of the galaxy,' he says, 'and that might arrive tomorrow. It might contain instructions to build something, or be full of information that we can download. Until that happens, I'm going to keep an open mind, but reserve judgement, on whether there's intelligent life.'

'So you don't think there is life out there in the universe?'

'If we're talking about the entire universe then all bets are off, because the universe is so big we don't even know how big it is. But I think it's best to contain a discussion like this to life in our galaxy alone. If there is life in another galaxy, just over there, say the Andromeda Galaxy, it's millions and millions of years away. Even with a radio signal travelling at the speed of light, it would take millions of years to get here – we couldn't have a meaningful conversation because by the time we've sent a message and got one back, that's older than humanity has been a species. The timescales just blow your mind.'

'So you don't think I'm lying about what I saw – you just think that I was mistaken?' I ask.

'I don't for a second think that you're lying. I think you truly believe you saw something that you don't understand, and you don't have an explanation for it, and I don't have an explanation for what you saw. But I think there's plenty of things out there that we don't yet have

SHAUN RYDER

an explanation for that might end up being run of the mill or standard, or have a normal explanation that we just haven't found yet.'

I try and put it a different way to him. 'If you woke up tomorrow morning and it was 6 a.m. and pitch black, and you looked out of your window and over your house you saw a proper UFO, and you watched it and observed it, and then it shot off at 10,000 miles an hour, how would that change the way that you think?'

'It obviously would. You've always got to keep an open mind and you've always got to allow for the possibility that you were wrong about particular things that get disproved by new evidence. But until that day . . . what confuses me about UFOs is it always seems to be people like yourself, or some friends, that see something in the sky that they don't understand. But if there was a UFO, a crew of aliens inside a flying saucer or spaceship, why would you bother visiting just two or three people at one time? Why would you not come to Mexico City, where ten million people at the same time could see it and there would be thousands and thousands of iPhone pictures of that same thing? But it's always just a few people. I'm not saying anybody is lying. You've seen something that you truly believe is not of this world and you can't explain it, and I can't explain it. But until there's something which is seen by lots of people, independently, all at the same time, that cannot be explained in any other way, [only then will I] believe in spaceships visiting us.'

This last part of my UK road trip has unexpectedly

been one of the most bonkers parts of my whole UFO adventure, and I've met some fascinating people who've opened my eyes to new realms of ufology. Speaking with Lewis gave me hope that there's potential for even the most sceptical individuals to change their mind about UFOs, with time.

Coming Down from My Trip

GETTING BACK HOME at the end of my UFO trip, it's a bit like coming off tour with the band. I feel like I'm coming back down to Earth and back to normal life. What did I expect to get out of this? I'm not sure I expected to get anything concrete out of it. I wanted to go on a journey and meet a lot of interesting people and ask a lot of questions about what's out there, or what could be out there, and it was a trip. I thought I would see some weird stuff along the way, but I saw miles more weird shit than I expected – the footage that we saw in Chile of the craft buzzing around during the military display, the weird stormtroopers that were descending from the sky over Chile and, most of all, the thing that Pancho actually captured on film up at Colbún Lake, which we didn't identify but was certainly something weird flying above the Earth.

I've waited a long time to experience the excitement I felt during my first UFO encounter, and that incident made my journey to the other side of the planet feel well worth the effort. What pleased me was that my manager Warren and the film crew were all there, as all of them needed a bit of convincing, but none of them could come up with an explanation for what we caught on camera that night. To me it's common sense that there's life elsewhere in the universe and this was another sign of that. But I didn't really write this book or make the show for me – it was more for those people who remain sceptical, to try and get them to be a bit more open-minded.

The footage that we saw of the weird stormtroopers was even more bizarre, but on reflection I think they were something to do with us – I think they were humans, not humanoid figures, but they had some new technology that the rest of us don't know about yet. It was probably just some new sort of experimental gear that some military geezers were trying out. You wait and see, I bet in thirty years or so our military will end up dressed like that – it will be the standard combat gear.

I'm glad I went to Chile first. I'm not sure it's somewhere I'll be taking Joanne and the kids, but I think it was a knockout place to start my UFO mission. It's definitely the UFO capital of the world right now. Rodrigo Fuenzalida, the director of Chile's leading civilian UFO group, told us that, 'There is not a single family in Chile without at least one or two members who have experienced a sighting', and it was really refreshing for me to be somewhere where most people believed in UFOs, or at least had an open mind about things.

I was brought up Catholic, and I think that definitely has had an effect on my way of thinking, whether I like it or not. Because it was pushed into my head from when I was a little kid, there's still part of me at the back of my brain that believes if you commit suicide you don't go to heaven, which I know will seem a bit crackers to a lot of people. Which I suppose must mean I believe in heaven. In some capacity. But I think the whole idea of God and heaven is a bigger concept than we can comprehend as human beings at the moment. I don't necessarily believe in God as an old man with a silver beard who sits up there surveying everything.

I have also been reading a lot about intelligent design over the last couple of years. Some of the scientists who are bang into the idea of intelligent design reckon that it doesn't mean you can't still believe in God. My beliefs are a bit magpie-like, I suppose. I take a bit from different places, a bit from here and a bit from there, whichever bits seem to make sense to me, which I think more and more people do nowadays. They pick the various bits that make sense to them – it's a bit like a pick'n'mix when you go to the cinema, you know what I mean? You leave the bits behind that you don't fancy and pick out the bits that you do, stick them in your bag and you're away. If you ever see someone else at a pick'n'mix you might see them pick up pear drops or something and think, 'What have you picked that for? That's the last thing I'd go for', and the same is probably true with other people's beliefs.

A lot of us are conditioned, as we grow up, to believe things just because humans have believed them for centuries, even though new evidence that has been unearthed recently or new scientific discoveries may contradict those old beliefs. I really think the next big scientific breakthrough will be in our minds, allowing us to be more open-minded. In a lot of ways, the main thing that is holding back scientific advances is the constrictions of the human mind, our refusal to accept that things that we previously thought were impossible might actually be possible. Scientifically, it is more likely that there is other life out there in the cosmos than there is a God.

I think most people struggle to accept extraterrestrial life because it would blow their minds. It totally would. As humans, we like to think we're this amazingly developed race, and so intelligent, but in some ways we're so small time. In many ways, we're still almost living in the dark ages. We continue to fight all over the planet about religion, for fuck's sake. Waging wars over things that might or might not have happened thousands of years ago. Does that seem intelligent to you?

I also think the authorities know more than they are letting on. One of the first things that plenty of new leaders have done when they get into power, particularly US Presidents or British Prime Ministers, is to say, 'Right then, bring me the UFO files.' Sir Winston Churchill did it. He was obsessed. JFK did it. Obama did it. But like I said earlier, when they get into power they are then reluctant to discuss it. Obviously they might not be able to say anything because they might be bound by secrecy and all that, but with some of them it's almost like they try to airbrush history and deny the fact that they were interested in the first place. They just never mention it themselves, and if the topic's raised they try and slide off the subject as quick as they can.

They know. Trust me, they know. If I can see something from my back garden then, with all the technology they've got, they've also seen it. They know. They've known for years. Just because they don't tell you doesn't mean anything. Do you think they would trust you with that information? Listen, we've just had evidence from whistleblower Edward Snowden that the US government is spying on just about everyone and everything – not just other governments but you, through your Facebook account, emails and everything. They don't trust you. Fact. But you reckon they trust you enough to share all their secrets about space and possible UFOs? Come off it.

I also think maybe it's harder for people to believe the evidence or footage that we do have now that you can create some really weird shit with camera trickery and stuff. No matter how clear the footage is, or how obvious it is that there's something not of this Earth there, some people will always say, 'Nah, that's just created.' It's not like the old days of fake footage – you can do anything now, and people are so used to camera effects and stuff at the cinema that they're less likely to take stuff at face value. Even I can be a bit sceptical myself when I see footage on television or YouTube.

But it's different when you see something with your own eyes. You know that's not camera trickery then. When you have seen a craft with your own eyes, how could it have been faked? Even if somebody had built a model of a craft, it wouldn't be able to move at anything like the speed or have the agility of what I saw. Not if it was built by humans.

I do think there will be a big announcement one day. Whether it's in my lifetime, or my kids' lifetime, I don't know. I think they're scared to tell us exactly what is going on, and I can understand why. Your average member of the general public would shit it if the government came out and said UFOs exist. Even if they were told, 'Listen, it's fine, don't worry. They are coming here and visiting us on Earth, but they've been coming here for millions of years, so you've got nothing to worry about', they would still shit it. They'd start panicking that their minds and bodies were about to be taken over by these alien beings.

To me, it's common sense that there is life out there, and I think one day everyone will see that.

The truth is out there, and I for one am going to try and keep getting closer to it.